God Blesses You
Ascension Messages from Sanhia

God Blesses You

Ascension Messages from Sanhia

Michael Hersey
with Sanhia

www.lightspira.com

Other books by Michael Hersey:

Ascension Numerology, 2016

Published by: LightSpira, Sweden
www.lightspira.com

ISBN: 978-91-86613-33-4
First edition, 2017

Author:	Michael Hersey
Word Whisperer:	Ulla Lindgren
Book & Cover design:	Marie Örnesved
Editing:	Stella Hansen
Ascension Guidance:	Sanhia

"Today we will embark upon a course you have not dreamed of. But the Holy One, the Giver of the happy dreams of life, Translator of perception into truth, the holy Guide to Heaven given you, has dreamed for you this journey which you make and start today, with the experience this day holds out to you to be your own."

A *Course in Miracles*: Lesson 157:8

Contents

Michael's Introduction

I have been channeling Sanhia for over thirty years. If you want to know that story, you can read about it in *Ascension Numerology: A Love Letter from Your Higher Self*. The significant thing for you to know now is that I am a conscious channel. I am fully aware of everything that comes through me from Sanhia. That means it is possible to block things that are uncomfortable or haven't yet been integrated into my own life. Therefore, as my spiritual development has progressed, the channeling has become clearer and stronger. I could say that I am now fearless in allowing Sanhia's full intention to shine through.

For years I wanted to find a way to share in print the wonderful things Sanhia was saying, but the time was not ripe. In 2009 Sanhia encouraged me to start channeling a short monthly message to be emailed to people who were interested. Over time the messages became longer and deeper.

As we were finishing the work on *Ascension Numerology*, Sanhia let me know that the next project was to be a collection of the messages. Let me explain a little about the co-creation process that gives birth to these messages. In the beginning the messages were short, and I tried to keep Sanhia's language intact as much as possible. When my partner Ulla and I began serious editing on the numerology book, we found ourselves guided to make significant changes to Sanhia's wording. This effort began to bleed over into the work with monthly messages. For those of you who haven't heard Sanhia directly, it is quite an experience. He is spontaneous and, often repeating things for emphasis. Much of the communication is through the energy of his voice. This doesn't come through well when the words are read from print. Our job became one of not just transcribing, but of interpreting Sanhia's intent into a prose form. When it came to revising the old messages, we found that many of them required a great deal of rewriting. Sanhia also wanted us bring more of a sense of timelessness to them. He wants you to know that he is pleased with the final result.

Sanhia's Introduction

You are here in this body, in this world for only one reason, to realize your divine nature. You are a child of God; none of this is real; and your inheritance from God of total love, joy, and peace is yours for the asking. Ascension means the experiencing of your divinity. It is the conscious realization that you are the creator of your world, that you cannot be a victim, that you always exist, and that nothing outside of love is real. It is knowing that you are one with God and with Spirit. This may be a lot for you to digest in this moment. As you read these messages, you can allow this truth to slowly sink into your every cell. The following introduction is a wonderful place to begin. These messages are intended to be read and reread.

For some of you, the study and pursuit of spirituality is one of your favorite pastimes. You love to takes classes, read books, have sessions, and so on. But, I want to ask you a question, something that only you can answer. Be brutally honest with yourself. Is spirituality a hobby for you? Perhaps I should say more about what I mean by hobby. A hobby is something that you enjoy doing and like to use your spare moments for. For some this time is filled by music, dance, art, handicrafts, camping and the outdoors, gardening, boating, carpentry, or one of numerous other interests. It is a way to enjoy yourself and to express your passions. When I ask if spirituality is a hobby for you, I am asking you to access what place it holds in your life.

Here are some indicators that spirituality might be a hobby for you. Perhaps you pursue something, have fun with it, take some classes, play around with it, and after a time begin to lose interest. Let's say you begin with feng shui and switch your interest to tarot or perhaps to an art class. At any rate, you find your interest and enthusiasm are now focused on different pursuits. This may show that spirituality is a hobby. Another sign might be that you are working with a particular spiritual practice and it triggers some deep energy for you that is not comfortable to handle. If you decide that isn't the fun that you signed up for and let it go, finding, perhaps, another means of expressing your spiritual interest – spirituality may be a hobby for you. Perhaps you have many sticks in the fire, dabbling with this and that but not going too deeply into anything in particular. Another indication is that, like hobbies in general, spirituality is a sideline for you. It is not something that is the forefront of your mind day-in and day-out. You focus on it some evenings or weekends, but day-to-day it is business as usual, with your focus on the "real world".

If you consider all of this with "brutal" self-honesty and say "Yes, that is how it is for me and I like it that way", we say "Fine" and we want you to enjoy this hobby and pursue it as fully as you desire. I will warn you that you will likely continue to see yourself as a victim. Your life will probably not live up to what you truly want it to be. If your response is that some of this is true for you, but you are not sure how you feel about it, let's discuss it a little further. If you want to experience, spiritual growth or – beyond that, realize your ascension – spirituality as a hobby will never get you there. If it is a sideline for you, there will only be marginal changes in your life. Is that fine with you? If so, that is wonderful, but you probably won't have an interest in reading further.

If you are saying to yourself that you want to experience more, to transform your life, you may want to revisit your "spirituality as a hobby" patterns. If your pattern is to move on when the newness of a spiritual interest wears off, try staying with it. Follow it deeper. Perhaps that means dropping some pursuits so that you can really focus on a few or even just one. There was a previous message that explained how the ego likes to divide and conquer (see Message 66). What draws you the most? Focus your energy. If a spiritual direction begins to threaten the ego, reasons will be suggested to move on to something different. When you stay with a spiritual practice, things will eventually be uncovered that you would rather not look at. This is the point you have wanted to reach if you have expressed the desire to transform your life. This is your gift. This is the place to face your fear and walk into it. This is where your spiritual pursuit is upgraded from a hobby into your life. This is the magic moment.

Now is the time when you decide to put your spiritual development on center stage. It is no longer related to the sidelines, to the weekends. It is no longer a bit player, but the star of the show. Your path becomes a daily focus. You are aware of it when you wake up in the morning. As you go through your day you try to bring awareness into each moment. It is the last thing you meditate on at night. You are not always successful at holding the focus, but that is your intention. Everything now takes a spiritual perspective. Perhaps this brings about the dropping of activities, relationships, or goals from your life. Everything will transform, whether it stays or leaves. Your deepest relationships become those where you can share your spiritual path. The energy around your job will alter, or you will find a new work. In like manner, your other hobbies will transform or begin to drop out of the picture. All of this can be quite scary. Putting spirituality in the spotlight will position you face to face with your worst fears.

This brings us to the second question. The first question was "Is spirituality a hobby for you?" The second question is "Have you made a clear commitment to realizing your ascension or your divine nature?" If not, you can be caught in a kind of "no man's land", a DMZ (DeMilitarized Zone) between hobby and commitment. This can be a rather uncomfortable place. You've left behind the seeming security of "spirituality as a hobby", but you don't have the strength that comes from intention and the support from Spirit to deal with the challenges that will come. You are stuck in the middle. It is not uncommon to have a lag time between leaving the hobby status and making a clear commitment. That intention does look frightening, and the ego has many reasons to convince you not to go all of the way. It looks like you have to let go of absolutely everything in your life. We are not saying that you should commit. You will know when it is time. Before that it would be a lie to you and to God. However, in the meantime you will likely face challenges that feel beyond your ability to handle.

My purpose is to support you in being perfectly clear about where you are and what you are choosing. You have three options:

1. Spirituality as a hobby
2. Spirituality being put on center stage
3. Absolutely committing to realizing your divinity.

What does commitment mean? Commitment means that you say to Spirit:

"I want you to support me in fully realizing my divinity. I want you to bring whatever changes that would best support that realization into my life. I want you to help me to change my thinking about absolutely everything until I am fully aligned with God. I want you to support me in seeing the divinity in not only myself, but in everybody. I want you to support me in forgiving every judgment I have, I want you to support me in seeing the perfection of every moment. I want you to support me in receiving everything that comes my way as an absolute gift. I want you to support me in choosing You over the ego in every moment."

I will warn you that once you fully commit, there may not be any way to go back to what seemed like safer places. The only way out may be to go forward and through it. However, your commitment allows you to do just that. Putting spirituality on center stage encourages all your fears to come creeping out of the dark. Committing to Spirit gives you the tools to fully deal with them. The fears aren't real, but you are. Wherever you are in the three stages, I am absolutely with you, as is Spirit, as is God. There is no judgment, only loving support. All you have to do to feel that support is to say "I will take it". The voice of Spirit will always guide you home.

Working Instructions

Here are a few suggestions for how to use this book. Of course you are free to do whatever you are guided to do, but simply reading through from cover to cover in a few days is not likely to bring you the greatest benefit. The following are a few ideas you can keep in mind:

1. Read just one message at a time. Over the following days, contemplate, reread, and meditate upon the message. See if there is any action you are guided to take. The messages are arranged chronologically, but it isn't necessary for you to follow them in that order. However, some concepts are introduced and then further developed in later messages. Sometimes when that occurs there is a reference to look back to the earlier message.

2. On the next four pages is a listing of nine major themes which are dealt with in depth in the book. Each has four sub-themes attached to it. You can find a theme that you are drawn to and read all of the messages that pertain to it.

3. There is an index of terms on page 254. The message numbers where those terms are used is noted. As you are reading, you will notice that each index term has a light dotted line drawn underneath it.

4. Directions for the *five-step process* are given on p. 230.

5. The earlier messages are shorter, but provide a good introduction to my spiritual perspective. The later messages give a deeper, perhaps more thought provoking insight.

6. The purpose of every message is to encourage you to realize your divine nature and to experience your ascension.

God Blesses You

Sanhia

Major Themes

One way to dive deeper into the ascension teachings of Sanhia is through investigating different themes that he covers. On the following pages, nine major themes found in the book are identified, each one accompanied by four related sub-themes. You can scan that list to see if there are any that particularly attract your attention. On p.232 you will find a list of messages that deal with each theme in a significant way.

Ascension
*The reason you are here; realizing your divinity,
your oneness with God*

- Release blame directed at yourself or others, the most important step to take toward realizing your ascension (*Forgiveness*)
- Everything that happens to you is perfectly designed to support your ascension (*Perfection*)
- You set up this lifetime with the intention to ascend (*Pre-planning*)
- Do what you came here to do; this aligns you with your ascension (*Purpose*)

Creation
Everything in your world is your manifestation

- Stay with your intention until it manifests or changes (*Commitment*)
- Creation comes after you decide what you want to manifest and communicate it to Spirit (*Intention*)
- Manifestation is the intersection of love and intention (*Power*)
- Whatever is in your life comes from you (*Responsibility*)

Divine Nature
You are the image of God, a being of unconditional love and unlimited creativity

- God offers you everything without any effort on your part (*Deservedness*)
- Innocence is your true and constant state, the way in which God sees you (*Innocence*)
- The ascended master Jesus models our divine nature for us (*Jesus*)
- You are one with God (*Oneness*)

Fear
An insane response to a non-existent threat, the cause of all suffering

- Ego is a terrified voice you listen to that thinks you are separate from God, and doesn't believe in your divinity (*Ego*)
- The *five-step process* helps you transform fear into love (*Five-Step Process*)
- *Spiritual Alchemy* is the transmuting of fear into love (*Spiritual Alchemy*)
- A spiritual perspective of world events contradicts fear (*World Events*)

Judgment
Believing there is such a thing as right and wrong, deciding what and who fits in either category

- Accept *what is* to release judgment (*Acceptance*)
- You judge yourself for having done something wrong, and so need punishing (*Guilt*)
- What you judge in another, you judge in yourself (*Mirror*)
- Judgment comes from the belief in right and wrong (*Right and Wrong*)

Love
Truth, the natural state, God, all you need

- Know that everything that comes into your life is a present for you assisting you in realizing your divine nature (*Gift*)
- Feel thankful for everything that happens to you, grateful for everything God has lovingly given you (*Gratitude*)
- Let love direct you, follow your inner drive (*Passion*)
- Do the loving service you came to perform (*Right Livelihood*)

Physical Body
You are not your body

- You believe falsely that you need something or someone in order to be happy (*Attachment*)
- All *dis-ease* is of your creation, good health is your birthright (*Health*)
- Home nurtures you if it truly is (*Home*)
- Balance the physical world's two poles (*Masculine and Feminine*)

Separation
False belief that keeps you stuck in hell

- Christianity preaches there is separation between you and God, failing to comprehend the true teachings of Jesus (*Christianity*)
- In separation you perceive things that don't exist, such as the world, fear, and death (*Illusion*)
- In separation you believe the world is real (*Reality*)
- Separation can be bridged through trust and faith (*Trust and Faith*)

Story
Personal belief that creates your "reality"

- Societal beliefs that run your life (*Mass Consciousness*)
- Life is just a picture show, it's your movie (*Movie*)
- Relationships are to support your spiritual growth (*Relationships*)
- The false story that things can happen to you without your permission (*Victimhood*)

What is true thankfulness?

When Americans think of November, their thoughts eventually turn to the Thanksgiving holiday. However, thankfulness is a state of mind I encourage everyone to hold in all seasons and under all circumstances. It may be easy to feel gratitude when surrounded by the bounty of the harvest and your loved ones, but it is equally important to feel grateful when plans and hopes and dreams fall through, when loved ones are lost.

True thanksgiving is in knowing and trusting the perfection of each moment. It lies in the recognition that even though we may not know why or how, we have asked for what we have received. We have done this to help us recognize the truth of who we are, the truth of reality. What we seek above all else is the knowingness of our divinity, our place as the unconditionally loved child of God. This holiday I encourage you to accept your gifts and to know that you deserve far more, but I also urge you to welcome the setbacks, to thank them for being there and to ask them to help lead you to a deeper understanding of the truth of your divinity and your eternal soul.

A suggested mantra:

Everything is perfect.

I welcome everything that comes to me today and I am grateful for this connection to my divine self.

God Blesses You,

Sanhia

What is the most valuable gift to give?

The celebration that you call Christmas has roots that go back far before the birth of Jesus. And, of course, as many of you know it is not even Jesus' birthday; he was a Pisces. The date was originally a celebration of renewal and hope, as this is the time of year when the sun finally begins its return and the days begin to grow longer. There will once again be a time when the earth bursts forth with green, with flowers, and finally with food.

In a sense, this is a holiday that reminds us of our deep inner knowing of our immortality. No matter how dark and cold things might appear to us in the illusion, in truth, there is always hope…there is always life. Many of you were raised with the knowledge of the Christian trinity of faith, hope, and charity, and that is certainly what this season is about.

- Faith…. trusting that everything is and always will be perfect, fine, and safe.

- Hope…. as we have just discussed, even in the deepest darkest days knowing that the darkness is illusion and that the light is behind it.

- Charity…. giving of ourselves without measure.

This trinity provides the watchwords for all time and places, but we choose to focus on them in particular during the Christmas season through creating more time and space to be outside of regular schedules – spending more time with family and friends, and with the rituals of gift giving. The most valuable gift through this season, and indeed throughout the year, is yourself. Truly be there for others, listening to their needs and desires, and giving with a faith and trust in your infinite supply of energy, time, and sustenance. With each person that you encounter – whether they be familiar or a stranger, friend or imagined enemy – look to see what you can give to them, whether it be a smile, an encouraging word, a meal, money, your ear, or your physical assistance. Mark out for yourself on your calendar Twelve Days of Christmas. Try practicing the dharma of unconditional giving during this time. You will find this gift is one that will always return to you in greater measure. Merry Christmas.

God Blesses You,

Sanhia

Will the earth survive?

Welcome to 2010! For many of you this is a milepost – the beginning of a new decade – and life is often measured by mileposts. For some of you there was a great concern about the milepost of 2000 or Y2K, the apocalyptic fears that the third millennium would be a disaster. I do not wish to treat these fears either too lightly or too heavily. This physical planet and your physical bodies are illusions and the truth of you is much grander and of course much more infinite. You could have chosen to end this experiment ten years ago, but the consciousness on the planet at that time voted to continue and to bring about the ascension of planet Earth.

Now, the fears are circulating about the magical year of 2012. According to the Mayan and Hopi calendars, 2012 is the end of time. Certainly, we have been experiencing the transition from the Piscean to the Aquarian age. Now, if you love the drama and feel that a world that is not in imminent danger of collapse is not worth living in, I know that you are enjoying yourself immensely. But for those of you who are experiencing some fear and would prefer not to, I have a few words for you. These prophecies of "the end" are predictions of the termination of business as usual. They are visions of the cessation of fear ruling the planet, auguries of the advent of love as the dominant energy. Change is often not smooth, but by choosing to release fear in your life on a daily, on an hourly, on a moment-to-moment basis – and replacing it with trust and love – you can avoid most of the gyrations of this planetary evolution.

It is truly the dawning of the Age of Aquarius. By the way, the lyrics to that song should not be written off as youthful idealism, but accepted as a prophecy. Are we ready? We affirmed the planet we wished to manifest at that time, and have spent the ensuing period healing those things within each of us that are not aligned with the dream. We have passed the point of no return. 2012 marks the time where there will be enough alignment with the dream to accelerate the transformation into an ascended earth. I encourage you again to choose love over fear, to know that the planet now supports your ascension in a more powerful way than has ever been experienced.

The signs may not be evident to your eyes, but you can feel the support inside of you. Remember that you are loved unconditionally, that you are divine, immortal children of God.

- Take deep breaths.
- Relax and enjoy this new decade.

God Blesses You,

Sanhia

Are there ghosts or evil spirits?

A question has come in about dealing with evil spirits or energies such as ghosts. There are several levels from which to approach this question, but let us start by focusing on basic truth. We shall begin with an understanding of who we are and how we operate in these physical bodies on planet Earth. We are children of God created in His image. That is to say we are immortal beings of infinite love and creativity. Each of us is unique and yet part of the divine whole or oneness. In creating and inhabiting our physical bodies we forget the truth of our beingness. It is part of our path to remember that the truth of who we are is divine love.

Anything that does not come from unconditional love is not real. The only thing that is true is love; anything that comes from fear or hatred is illusory. Whatever might threaten us is unreal. There is nothing ultimately that can harm the truth of who we are. This is not to say that the physical body cannot experience harm, but our true selves are eternal and indestructible.

It is time now to deal with the next level, that of the planet Earth being a realm of free choice. We are able through our thought processes and emotions to create any possible experience on earth. First of all, it is important to acknowledge that our experiences are our creations, that by the very nature of who we are we cannot be the victims of any other being's energy. Another being can only give us the illusion of harming us if we give it permission to do so. We do create the reality we experience in these bodies.

If you are experiencing fear that a ghost or any other entity, including one in a physical body, might do you harm there are clear steps to take. First, remind yourself of your divinity, of your oneness with God, of your immortality. Remember that there is only love, that all else is illusion. Affirm that you are safe, that no outside energy or entity can affect you without your permission. State that you do not give your consent for any entity to harm you. Request that your guides or Spirit protect you from any unwanted outside influence. You are in charge here. Nothing can violate your physical body without your agreement.

At this point in the message it is likely that your mind is reacting with a variety of questions and doubts, and this is fine. I am not suggesting that people have consciously chosen their suffering through the ages, only that the beliefs that they hold allowed these events to transpire. Even today there are many who believe that the greatest gift they can give to mankind is the sacrifice of their lives. God has never asked for such an atonement, but holds no judgment for whatever choices are made by those in the "human condition". I wish you to hear the humor in my voice as I say "the human condition". By this term, I mean simply the believing of self to be separate from the infinite Creator.

One more level that I wish to address is for those of you who may wish to take action to support the ghost or entity or person that might be perceived as threatening. First repeat silently the four statements, "I love you", "thank you", "please forgive me", and "I'm sorry" over and over. Ask silently what the entity wants in order for it to feel at peace. Using your knowledge of the nature of reality, guide the entity to choose that possibility for itself. Remind it that it is loved and is a divine child of an infinitely and unconditionally loving God.

Know that you are safe and unconditionally loved.

God Blesses You,

Sanhia

Can I follow my passions?

I would like to talk about passion. It is the term I use to describe the feminine energy. Passion is the way that you focus your love to manifest in the world. The masculine energy, expressed by the mind, has the task of holding a clear image of where you wish to go, accentuating the positive. But it is your passion that determines what that vision is. Your passion is what connects you to your purpose.

There is the generalized purpose, shared by all beings, to ascend, that is, to remember the truth of who you are and to experience that truth as infinitely creative, loving, forgiving children of God. Yet, even as you are all one and connected, you are also unique and individual. You each have your irreplaceable role to play. This is your specific purpose. How do you find out what it is? By trusting, listening to, and following your passion. This would never be experienced as something you have to or must do. Rather, you have a deep desire to do it. The task at hand is to listen to these aspirations without judgment, to believe that you deserve to have them fulfilled even when the mind says that these yearnings are petty and selfish. It is not for you to judge your passions, but simply to give intention for their fulfillment.

Passion is blocked by fear. Fear is old energy. It is a combination of feeling undeserving, guilty, and powerless. It is feeling yourself to be a failure. This fear can block the ability to act on or to even hear your passions. It becomes the job of your masculine side to "create a protected place for his lady". The mind is to affirm that it is safe to experience your passion, that you deserve to manifest what you desire. Your mind affirms that you have the ability to manifest your dreams and reminds you that you are innocent, that God loves you unconditionally and supports your every choice.

You do not need to understand the part that your passion plays in the larger picture. It is only for you to trust that your role is of divine importance and that it can only be fulfilled by listening to and following your passion.

God Blesses You,

Sanhia

What is the most appropriate way to honor Jesus?

Perhaps one of the subjects that is of greatest interest to those of you in the Western spiritual traditions is the Jesus lifetime. I wish to make a disclaimer explaining my point of view in relation to Jesus. In that lifetime, I was known as Thomas, who has subsequently been saddled with the nickname "Doubting Thomas". I recorded some of the commentaries of Jesus. The fathers of the Roman Catholic Church in the 3rd and 4th centuries chose to omit that text from what was called the New Testament and made attempts to destroy all copies. As many of you already know, one of the copies has survived and, though it is a later copy with additions and deletions made to the original, there is still much of value to be found in what is called the Gospel of Thomas. Lastly, as to Thomas, some of you may be aware of others who trace their lineage to this apostle. Understand that it is common for beings to manifest what could be called splinter personalities or multiple reincarnations of the same entity.

But let us return now to Jesus. He came here to teach us about ascension and he manifested it in a very public way so that it would be recorded for posterity, even if incompletely understood. What is important for us to comprehend about Jesus is that, yes, he is the son of God, but that you and I are also the sons and daughters of God. We are all one. One of the greatest confusions in Christianity as a religion is the separation of Jesus from the rest of humanity. As Jesus said, "This and more you shall do." Jesus was not the first to ascend, but it was part of his purpose to show us the way. That way consists of unconditional love, affirming oneness with the Creator, forgiveness, acceptance, and the release of judgment. Jesus modeled unconditional love in a manner that was transformational for those of us who were around him. He saw others in their divinity, in their perfection. As people allowed themselves to be enveloped in this unconditional acceptance and forgiveness they found themselves healed, physically and spiritually.

The most appropriate way to honor Jesus is to use him as a model for your own life, neither exalting him above you nor lowering him to a "human" level. Love and forgive yourself and others unconditionally. Accept your place as the innocent child of God, and choose and affirm your ascension. It is not necessary to proselytize the teachings of Jesus, but as you live a life of unconditional love you will draw to yourself those who wish to learn from you.

God Blesses You,

Sanhia

Do I deserve to have my desires fulfilled?

We have spoken about passion. Many questions have come from you on this topic, so we will take another leap into it. Some of you in your spiritual training have learned that suffering is the result of desires. Let's begin there. I would like to classify desires into two categories which could be called "lower" desires and "higher" desires. The term "lower" is not intended to express judgment, but to merely be descriptive. "Lower" desires are pleasing to the senses and have a more immediate pull on the heart. These might include (but are certainly not limited to) enjoying food and beautiful scenery, listening to music, dancing, drawing, sculpting, walking, having sex, talking, and being with friends. "Higher" desires are often connected with Right Livelihood, the gifts you have to offer to others, your purpose, and ascension.

In those times when you feel blocked off from an awareness of what your "higher" desires are or of the possibility of ever fulfilling them, your "lower" desires exist to help open the doors to trusting the "higher" ones. The bottom line in being able to achieve any aspiration is the belief that you deserve to realize it. Whatever you feel desire for – nurture that feeling and affirm that you deserve to have it fulfilled, that as an innocent, divine child of God, it is your birthright. See it done in your mind.

You may have the fear that if you allow yourself to pursue all of your "lower" desires you will become bogged down in a selfish, hedonistic lifestyle. I wish to remind you that your desires or passions are the way that your God-self speaks to you. Addiction and the self-destructive pursuit of pleasure is the result of self judgment and guilt. Selfishness and greed grow from the belief that there is not enough; that, therefore, what you get must be taken from another. The work that is cut out for you is listening to your passion (both "lower" and "higher") and following it. Use your masculine side to affirm that there is an abundance of everything for everyone, that you deserve to have whatever comes to you, and that you are an innocent, loving child of God.

The opposite of acting out of passion is doing things because you "should" do them. It is just as important to begin to eliminate the "shoulds" from your life as it is to follow your passion. Each time you eliminate a "should" you create a space which you will want to guard carefully and fill only with a desire. For some of you your biggest "should" is your job. You have a passion to do something else but keep your current position out of fear. Your voices say, "How will I survive without this job", or "Being a responsible adult means going to a work every day", or "I need health insurance." Here we would speak of "lower" and "higher" desires. Sometimes it is easier to focus on the "lower shoulds", the little places where you say yes, but feel a no. These are perhaps the areas to begin to focus your energies, to remind yourselves that you deserve to do the things you wish to do, and that you are entitled to enjoy your life. You may have to begin by having the courage to change little things before you are ready to confront the larger ones, such as unfulfilling jobs or relationships. Sometimes by transforming the smaller issues the larger ones handle themselves. In other words, as you follow a discipline of obeying your "lower" desires and saying no to the little things, you may begin to experience that your job has improved and that your relationships give you greater satisfaction. You deserve it all.

God Blesses You,

Sanhia

Why is forgiveness important?

We have spoken about forgiveness with many of you before, but it is a topic that cannot be overdone. Forgiveness could be a daily focus; it is central to all healing. When you hold a grudge or you extend blame toward another or yourself, you block the flow of love from moving freely through your life. Blame and its shadow side, guilt, always are generated by fear, not by love. They are illusions and not the truth. When you blame another, you take the role of victim; you live in the pretense that you are weak and not the author of your experience.

Let us return to the truth of who you are. You are a divine child of God. You are an immortal, infinitely creative, and unconditionally loved being. You chose to believe that you could create separate from your Creator. This was an illusion; all is one and cannot be divided. Your Creator continues to see you in truth, unconditionally loving and accepting you, but you choose to judge yourself for this separation and to feel guilt and a need for forgiveness and atonement. You created this physical incarnation as a place to heal the guilt and separation.

When it comes to forgiving another, it helps to remember that there is nothing to forgive, that everything in this earth plane is an illusion. The event that is troubling you is your creation intended for your healing. The other people involved in your event are there because you set up their involvement. The aspect of them that is divine agreed to help you out. Nobody is at fault. As you fully realize this, forgiveness is easy because there truly is nothing to forgive. The event is a manifestation of your belief that you need to be forgiven, but God only sees you in your innocent perfection. There is nothing to forgive.

As you run into judgments of yourself and others repeat to yourself (these statements are graciously borrowed from Ho'oponopono):

- I love you...... (As God always loves you)

- Forgive me.... (It is only yourself who can forgive and let go)

- I'm sorry....... (I'm sorry for choosing fear instead of love)

- Thank you.... (Thank you for reminding me that there is only love)

God Blesses You,

Sanhia

What is confused in Christianity?

Many of you are Christian or come from a Christian background. Sometimes this causes confusion as your spiritual path opens and develops. I would like to help you separate the wheat from the chaff. The things that may confuse you about Christianity (if not outright run you off) probably did not come from Jesus. As one of his former right-hand people (there were two dozen of us), I would like to try to set the record straight about ten common confused "Christian" beliefs. There is a lot here. Meditate on any that aren't clear to you.

1. *If you sin, you will go to hell.*
Hell does not exist except in the mind. God loves unconditionally, does not judge, and of course would never condemn. Hell is a creation of the children of God, is fear-based, and is therefore not real. People who live in fear may be experiencing an illusion of hell, but the only thing that is eternal is love.

2. *Jesus died for our sins.*
Jesus left his body at the conclusion of his personal ascension process. He was able to ascend because he loved everyone unconditionally. If we define sin as the belief that we are separate from and judged by God, Jesus along with us was a sinner. His departure from his physical body marked the total release of his sin, or his belief in his own separation from the divine. Certainly, his ascension supports us in ours.

3. *Jesus is the Son of God.*
Yes, he is, but so are you. We are all one. Jesus never said, "I am the Son of God, but you aren't". No, he said, "This and more you shall do." Jesus is like an older brother who has shown us the ropes. He is not someone who is different from us; he simply matured (ascended) earlier. This is not to downplay the enormity of his gift, only to remind you that you will get there, too.

4. *Jesus suffered for us.*

The vision of extreme pain and suffering, which had dominated the story as told by both Catholic and Protestant churches, is a projection painted from a human, separated, fear-based position. Jesus did not experience pain on the cross. He felt unconditional love for everyone involved. Pain is fear-based; unconditional love experiences only bliss.

5. *The Bible is to be taken literally.*

Warnings exist in the Bible not to worship graven images. What is the Bible if not a graven (engraved) image? We could nitpick and talk about how the original texts were in Aramaic or Greek and how something is always lost in the translation, or that even the English versions differ. But what is more important is realizing that these stories were written by people; God has no horse in this race. These stories were sometimes inspired by the teller's higher self/ divine guidance. Your job is to follow your own intuition when reading scripture. If it feels inspired by love, trust it. If it feels fear-based, it probably isn't guidance for you today.

6. *Christianity is the only path to salvation.*

All roads lead to ascension. In the last analysis, ascension is a very personal and private thing. No two people will follow the exact same path. The teachings of those who have come before you are for your enlightenment and support, but the farther you come on your path, the more you are on your own (your connection to infinite love). Any religion is as good an entry place as another.

7. *There is no such thing as reincarnation.*

Yeah, you thought that your last lifetime, too. Seriously, this physical plane and the physical body are illusions. They only thing that is real and eternal about you is your soul, your spirit. You created the earth plane to help you heal your separation from God. There is no final judgment. There is not even a starting line. You create each incarnation with what you can use to reach ascension. Or maybe you just came in this time to serve another. Either way, you have unlimited shots (and don't forget that time is an illusion, too).

8. *Homosexuality is wrong and sinful.*
Let's all repeat the following ten times: "God has no judgment". Good. Forgiveness is the key to ascension. Releasing all judgments is central to your healing process.

9. *Only men can become spiritual leaders.*
As some of you already know there were 24 disciples, not 12. We each had a female counterpart. Jesus, of course, had Mary Magdalene, who also ascended. Male spiritual leaders have been more prominent because this male dominated planet has had less respect for women. Meanwhile, let your inner guidance lead you to the voices that inspire you. Reproductive organs have nothing to do with it. Gender is an illusion, also. Your divine self is neither male nor female.

10. *There is such a thing as a righteous (Christian) war.*
I challenge anybody to find a quote attributed to Jesus that supports war. He talked about love, loving your neighbor, turning the other cheek. There is nary a word even about self-defense. This being said, there is to be no judgment of war, simply the realization that it is fear-based, not loved based, and not a part of the ascension path.

God Blesses You,

Sanhia

Is there a conflict between politics and spirituality?

It is election season in the United States. That reminds me of something Jesus said, "Render unto Caesar what is Caesar's". I would like to do a deeper interpretation of this statement. Politics has become quite divisive in the United States. Perhaps it has always been that way, but the level of opposition is intensifying. How many of you have demonized the political opposition, whether individually or en masse?

Many of you sense where this is going and are already complaining under your breath, "Aw Sanhia, can't we have some righteous indignation?" Well that depends. Are you the victim of your political opponents? Do they control your life? Or are you a divine child of God, infinitely powerful and unconditionally loving? You create your own reality. Why would you choose to give that power away to your political enemy? Why indeed would you choose to have a political enemy, knowing that everyone is simply your mirror? Whatever that political figure plugs you in to, is what you are judging yourself for. Thank them for keeping you on your spiritual toes. Transform the triggered anger and judgment by using the *five-step process* (see p. 230). Believing that salvation lies in the political system is a denial of reality. Your salvation lies totally within you. Render unto Caesar whatever you must, but do it joyfully, and don't give up your power. Practice doing Ho'oponopono (see Message 8) on the politicians and the pundits.

I am not suggesting that there is no value in becoming politically active. Follow your passion. If a candidate shares your vision, run with it. Support a positive future for the planet. I am only warning you about dwelling on the negative. Choose love always over fear. But, remember that Jesus did not come here to become king. Planetary ascension happens as individuals move toward and into ascension. It is not a product of political battles.

Practice loving everyone on the political stage unconditionally. Oh! And don't forget to vote (if you want to). Smiles.

God Blesses You,

Sanhia

Can I love myself into ascension?

How many of you are successful at being your own worst critic? This is often touted as a valuable skill for those on the spiritual path. It is a common belief that by being able to notice your alleged shortcomings, you are better able to heal and to grow. I wish to go on record as the loyal contrarian. Certainly, what you judge in another is what you judge in yourself, but the question is not how to better notice your faults, but how best to stop judging yourself.

My suggestion is to think of what you would like to hear your best friend (an imaginary best friend, if that helps) say to you as you are judging yourself. What wonderful thing would you like to hear them say about you? Say whatever you would like to hear from your best friend. Say it to yourself. Become your own best friend. That's the message. It's short and sweet. Be your own best friend. Give up the "no pain, no gain" philosophy and love yourself into ascension.

Be your own best friend.

God Blesses You,

Sanhia

Will I ever fully heal myself?

Have you been working on your personal healing for years? Have you been doing a lot of "processing"? Does it sometimes feel like there is an infinite amount of crap in there for you to clean up? Past lives, birth trauma, parents, bullies, self-worth issues, relationships, authority figures, the opposite sex, sexuality, purpose.........when will it ever end? The answer is that it will never end. As long as your focus is on healing your problems, there will be problems.

What do I do, Sanhia? Just give up? That would be a good start, but let me give it a little different focus. All this concentration on healing comes from the belief that there is something (many things!) wrong with you and that you need to be fixed. My job is to remind you that you are perfect; that there is nothing to heal; that you are a divine and innocent child of God. You did not create this body in order to heal; you created it so that you could realize your divine nature.

You are here to love. This could be stated in a variety of ways. You are here to follow your passion, to express, and to be joyful. You are here to love yourself and others, and to give joyful, devoted service. You are here to fully realize the truth of who you are as a divine and innocent child of God.

Choose fun. Choose love. Choose what you want. 'Tis the season to choose to be jolly (as are all of the others).

God Blesses You,

Sanhia

How can I get more joy in my life?

This will reach many of you on New Year's Day. Some of you will be making resolutions, so let me jump on that bandwagon. I want to encourage you to make a resolution to commit to joy.

"What does this mean, Sanhia?" you may be thinking. Remember, it is your passion that connects you to your God-self and it is following your desires that brings you happiness. At the micro-level in each moment, choose the action or the thought that brings you more pleasure. This cannot be predicted in advance; that is, you can't make a schedule for yourself and trust that it will adhere to the guideline of following your passion. You may have a loose idea of what you would like to accomplish today, but committing to joy may require you to be eternally vigilant to what is burning within you in the moment, and then flow through the day from one thing to another.

In a given moment you may be conscious of feeling a need to attend to something that you do not have excitement for. Simply be aware that you are making that choice. Ask Spirit that the action be experienced as pleasurably as possible and that it lead you in a serendipitous way to increased bliss.

By starting with small choices, you can gradually work your way to the larger choices that will increase your joy. You don't need to quit your job or leave your relationship today. If it is truly time to do something like that, you will know. In the meantime, find the small actions throughout the day that make the job or the relationship more enjoyable.

Be conscious also about how you are spending money. How many purchases are habit based rather than joy based? Check to see if you truly have passion in that moment for the purchase you are making. Credit can sometimes numb your ability to perceive what your desires truly are. If you are having credit problems, you might want to try buying only with cash (or check or debit card). See what you want most with the funds you actually have.

Commit to joy. Commit to passion. Commit to ascension. Who would want to live in a joyless eternity? Your commitment to joy will prepare you well for whatever awaits you.

God Blesses You,

Sanhia

What can I do when I feel like a victim?

For many of you the month of February can be the most difficult of months. You are through with winter, but winter is not through with you. Maybe the most positive thought you can come up with is, "Thank God for only giving us 28 days this month". I would like to spread a little light into this cavern.

To begin with, I want to remind you that there is no such thing as a victim. Victimhood is an illusion, but the tighter you hold on to it, the more real it seems.

Repeat after me:
- I am not a victim.
- I am an innocent, totally lovable, infinitely creative child of God.
- I create everything in this physical realm.
- Nothing can appear here without my permission.
- Everything that I do create is with the intention of bringing me closer to the complete awareness of who I truly am.
- Therefore, everything that happens is perfect.
- My mantra is, "This is perfect".

This is not a tease. Are you willing to try it? When the car won't start? This is perfect. When things don't go as you want them to at work? This is perfect. When you have a fight with someone you love? This is perfect. When your finances trouble you? This is perfect.

- Affirm perfection. Do what you can do. Let it go.

It is not necessary to consciously know why it is perfect. That knowledge will come to you in its own perfect time. Trust that it is perfect. Feel that it is perfect. Then you will know that it is perfect.

God Blesses You,

Sanhia

What was the Arab Spring about?

Many of you are aware of some of the changes that have been going on in North Africa. While I don't spend a lot of time watching the macro events of the day (I am much more concerned with your individual ascension process), sometimes Michael tugs my chain and wants to know what is going on in the world. This process in the Muslim realm is most interesting, and is, of course, a manifestation of the inner work that is going on worldwide. All religions are one; that is, they all offer equal opportunities to foster personal transformation or, on the other hand, present opportunities for giving away power to others.

What we have going on in Egypt, Tunisia, Libya, and other countries are large numbers of people simultaneously getting that they don't need to give away their power anymore. Leaders who have ruled through fear are finding out that fear is no longer working. Does this mean that love will suddenly rule throughout the region? Not likely, but the genie is out of the bottle. As in your personal process, there is still a lot of fear to be released. There is always the danger of replacing the old masters with new masters.

Where does all of this leave you? First, I suspect, filled with some sense of excitement and possibility. If these people who face death for their rebellion against the old ways have found the courage to set themselves free, why not we? Few of you have a literal gun at your head. Is it time to take the leap of faith? Is it time to say "no" to the inner fear demons? Is it time to claim your passion and really go for it? The energy of the planet is with you. Mountains are moving.

I would like to go on record as saying, "Go for it!"

God Blesses You,

Sanhia

How can I protect myself from natural disasters?

Some of you have been concerned about the tsunami in Japan, whether about the death, the destruction, or the radioactive danger. Natural disasters are some of the most challenging concerns for the evolving consciousness to make peace with. I will not say anything here that I have not said before, but there is often an enormous gap between the hearing of something and the full integration of that idea into the cellular level, the absolute knowingness of its veracity. I will repeat:

1. There are no accidents. There are no victims. Everything that happens on this planet happens through conscious or unconscious human creation. If you have fear of what you might create unconsciously, give clear directions to Spirit. The world is your mirror. What do you wish to be looking at? Notice what your fear is and speak to it.
   - "I choose to remain protected from natural disasters."
   - "I choose to remain protected from man-made disasters."
   - "I choose to remain protected from terminal dis-eases."
   Finally do the *five-step process* (see p. 230).

2. You are immortal. Your physical body may die, but the truth of who you are can never be destroyed. Your unconscious may draw to you a life ending event, but the truth of you will remain untouched. You are always safe. Repeat:
   - "I am always safe."
   - You are an innocent unconditionally loved child of God, infinitely creative.
   - Your body is an illusion that you have created, as is the earth.

- What is real is the infinite love from which they were created.
- If it is not about love, it is not real.

3. Everything is perfect. Whatever happens is always the best thing that could happen. Your unconscious does not work against your best interests. On the contrary, it has to work around the mixed messages your conscious mind is sending in order to best bring you what your deepest desire is. Repeat: "Everything is perfect". Even though you are not aware in the present moment why something is perfect, it is still perfect. The understanding will likely come later, but allow the trust to be there now. Relax into the knowingness that there is only perfection.

Don't worry; be happy.

God Blesses You,

Sanhia

What does attachment mean?

For those of you not familiar with Buddhism, the Buddha left us the Four Noble Truths.

1. Everyone suffers.
2. Suffering comes from attachment.
3. There can be an end to suffering.
4. This end comes from following the Eightfold Path.

I am not going to go into the Eightfold Path today, but it is similar to things I have been sharing with you for years. Let us talk about attachment. It means having your emotional happiness, your peace of mind, dependent on things being the way that you want them to be, now. It might be attachment to the weather being a certain way or to a friend doing as you wish or to having more money or to getting the job you want. Whatever it is that is not the way you want it to be will bring you suffering unless you give up attachment. I wish for you to be free of suffering.

Giving up attachment does not mean giving up desire. It does not mean giving up passion. It works like this. You feel a passion for something. This is guidance from your higher self, your God self. You ask Spirit for support. Then you let it go. Your job is over, except for one small thing. You are to trust that the perfect thing is returning to you. It may not look exactly like what you thought it would. If you knew exactly what would bring about your ascension you would have requested it long ago. All you can do is ask for that part that is revealed to you, and let it go. Whatever is in your life today is the perfect response to your past requests. Give up struggling and accept. Trust the perfection of the moment.

Think about what you are doing when you are attached to things being different than they are. You are affirming your powerlessness and your victimhood. You are expressing your lack of trust in the Divine. This is not only how you are experiencing your present, but it is what you are projecting for your future.

Why struggle? Why make it hard? Just let go. It is so easy. Just let go. Just trust. Just surrender. Just relax. It is all perfect. There is a present here for you now, today. You can't open it; you can't receive it until you let go of what you thought would be there in its place. Open it now.

God Blesses You,

Sanhia

How can numerology support me on my ascension path?

Many of you have received numerology readings from Michael or from me. I would like to tell you more about numerology. Lao Tzu said that the Way that can be explained is not the true Way. Words can only approximate truth. Numbers are truth. The words used to explain those numbers are not truth, but the numbers themselves cannot lie.

Each number vibration has an essence about it. Words can attempt to narrow your mental understanding of that essence, but ultimately it is a truth that is felt. The same is true of the various positions that a numeric vibration might hold in a personal numerology chart. The true meaning of that position can be implied, but never fully explained. The real truth of the number in that position can also only be intuited, as can the relationships between vibrations in different positions.

Why is all of this important? It is valuable because it is a way that divine wisdom, your higher self, Spirit can speak directly to you. There are no accidents in the universe. Your name is not the truth of who you are, but it represents the truth of what you came to do. Your birthday tells about the events that your higher self is creating so that you can realize your purpose here.

This information is not always comfortable to receive, but it is rarely truly surprising. Seek the truth, for it shall set you free. Receiving a reading is like being fed the proverbial fish. It will feed your spiritual growth for today. Become conversant in the numerological dialogue and you can feed yourself forever. There are many paths to truth and they are all blessed. This one I love because of its simplicity: nine vibrations, twelve major positions.

The energy is not written in stone; it is written in flesh. It does not command – this is still the planet of free choice – it only informs. The wise pay attention and learn from all that they create. Your wisdom will lead you to peace.

God Blesses You,

Sanhia

Why have religions been male dominated?

The monotheistic movement, the change from a belief in many gods to the belief in one God, was a most significant event – actually quite a stretched-out event – in the history of spirituality on earth. Though monotheism is true in spirit (pun intended), much is often lost in the translation.

The pagan gods that were outlawed by Judaism were often feminine. The monotheistic God was often perceived as male. This has led to religions that are male dominated. Even though Mary Magdalene ascended as well as did Jesus and each apostle had a female partner who was an equal part of the discipleship, only the males made it into the New Testament. Women have often been denied the role of spiritual leadership or have been delegated to a role as second class citizens due to interpretations of monotheistic scriptures.

Men didn't come out ahead in this. Part of the covenant that men were asked to make with the male God was to give up their masculinity to Him. They were to follow the dictates of the Father as translated to them by other men in the form of scriptures and the priesthood. In subconscious reaction to this, men have taken out their anger upon women, even blaming them for their "fall".

Let's look at the truth of gender and divinity. God has no gender. God is unconditional love and infinite creativity. Only your physical incarnation has gender. The truth of who you are as a child of God is gender-free. The pagan gods often were representative of the guides or angels or even the higher selves of humans in physical form. Truly, when you pray, affirm, or give intention for something – the response comes from Spirit. It may be communicated through guides/angels who are also children of God and interact with the earth. God does not become directly involved with the actions on earth. He loves unconditionally. Earth is our creation and our responsibility.

Gender has an important part to play in the healing process you are going through on earth. But, like the body, it is an illusion and does not represent the truth of who you are. Do your best to visualize God as a divine light or as an infinite ocean or in any way that does not involve personification. You are always loved unconditionally. There is never any divine judgment. The point is approaching where the father images will be the farthest thing from your minds. You are divine.

God Blesses You,

Sanhia

Can you suggest a prayer for ascension?

As you are all aware, there is either love or fear in each moment of each life. Love is truth; fear is illusion – it is not real. The deep inner knowledge of love as truth is what is called faith. Those who live in faith, live in joy. The absence of fear is an ecstatic experience. Thomas Merton was a 20th century Trappist Monk who understood, lived, and communicated the truth of love and faith to a very high degree. I want to share with you a meditation or prayer he wrote (channeled) concerning faith.

"My Lord God, I have no idea where I am going. I do not see the road ahead of me. I cannot know for certain where it will end. Nor do I really know myself, and the fact that I think I am following Your will does not mean that I am actually doing so. But I believe that the desire to please You does in fact please You. And I hope I have the desire in all that I am doing. I hope that I will never do anything apart from that desire. And I know that if I do this, You will lead me by the right road, though I may know nothing about it. Therefore, I will trust You always though I may seem to be lost and in the shadow of death. I will not fear, for You are ever with me, and You will never leave me to face my perils alone." (from *Thoughts in Solitude*)

Allow me to interpret this into my terminology.

"Oh, Spirit, I have no idea where I am going. I do not see the road before me. I cannot for certain know where it will end. I still feel separate from you. I am following the guidance of my passions, but I'm not certain if I am guided by love or fear. I desire to be guided by unconditional love. I want to feel at one with you. I desire to be always aligned with my true passion. I desire to always listen to the voice of love rather than the voice of fear. I know that no matter which I choose you will lead me to the events that will best facilitate my healing, because I have asked for it. I know that everything that happens is perfect, even if I do not yet understand why. I trust that I am safe and protected no matter how great my fear may be. I know that I am never alone, that the truth of me is immortal and cannot be harmed, and that you and my guides are always with me."

You are always safe. Everything that happens is perfect. Follow your deepest passions. You are greatly and unconditionally loved.

God Blesses You,

Sanhia

Why should I take responsibility for what others do to me?

Some people have expressed concern that the concept of taking personal responsibility for what are seen as negative acts of others amounts to blaming the victim. There is fear that this takes responsibility away from the alleged perpetrator and indeed can be used as an excuse for others' "negative" actions. This line of thinking continues by suggesting that the actions of others won't change until they are held accountable for what they do.

Taking responsibility for everything that happens in your life is not about blame or about victimhood. It is about truth and it is about salvation. Either you are powerful and control your world (consciously or unconsciously), or you are a helpless victim of random events or the whims of a loving or not-so-loving God. If the latter is true it's time to circle the wagons and protect yourself the best you can, knowing anything might happen to you at any time. That choice can lead you to live in fear. True freedom from fear can only come from acknowledging the truth and embracing it.

The truth is very simple. You are a child of God and infinitely powerful and creative. You have forgotten this in the process of coming into a physical body. Healing is the process of remembering. Just because you have forgotten your true power or are denying it does not take away that power. It simply makes it difficult to use effectively or consciously. Used consciously, power combines love with a desired outcome to create your desired experience. Used unconsciously, power uses fear (expressed as any of a variety of negative emotions) to create the seemingly undesired. However, since the deepest desire of those on an intentional spiritual path is always to be healed, even the seemingly undesired is there to support in your healing. Spirit will always shower you with the gifts that nurture healing. The quickest route to healing or the state of always being in love is to own your power by taking responsibility for everything that happens in your life, knowing that you created it even if you don't understand how or why.

This does not mean you have to stick your head in the lion's mouth, but if you should find it there do not blame the lion. You have created that lion being there in order to help you move through the fear/judgment that separates you from love, from your higher self, from God. It is okay to choose to stay away from the lion, but if you do that out of the judgment that the lion is evil, you are choosing fear and not love. You have made your healing path that much harder and longer. Choose to stay away from the lion because you feel that in the moment you can heal faster or more easily when not in the lion's presence, knowing that it is you and not the lion that is to do the changing. Have the intention to one day be in the lion's presence with only love, without fear.

Because you are infinitely creative, everything that you experience in life is your manifestation. If you find yourself in judgment of what you see, it is yourself you are judging. If you take it as a gift, you can see where your healing is to begin. If you pretend that your judgment is truth, you deny your power and will continue to create the same types of events until there is a healing, until you take responsibility.

Because I care about you and want you to be in a place of experiencing love all of the time, I hope that you find it in your heart to practice only love and forgiveness for yourself and for others.

God Blesses You,

Sanhia

What is the first step toward realizing my ascension?

How many of you have made a clear intention for ascension? Nothing happens in the universe until you ask for it. Ask and it shall be given. Once you have stated your intention to to Spirit (guides, God, the universe, or whatever name you wish to give) nothing can stop it from happening. Nothing can stand between you and your intention but time. And time, as we all know, is an illusion.

You have other desires, in addition to your wish for ascension. These goals could be identified as higher or lower desires. This does not indicate a judgment, it is simply a question of whether the desire is connected to the truth of who you are or to enjoying your experience in a body. Higher desires might be connected to your purpose or to relationships or to healing. Lower desires might have to do with where you live, what you wear, what food you eat, or which experiences you wish to have. Have you given intention for them? I probably don't need to remind you not to ask for things that might bring harm or loss to others; not because there is any judgment about doing that, but because what you project on another, you also project on yourself. It all passes through you first. You will always receive the things that support you in the highest way toward knowing the truth about yourself, of realizing your divinity.

It is not necessary to ask over and over for the same thing. Once is sufficient. Once is all it takes to put things into motion. Spirit will not act, however, without your permission. This is the planet of free will. Nothing has the power to overcome your will without your expressed permission. You must start the ball rolling. If you have already done that, it is time to trust. Know that your answer is coming to you. Look for it in everything that comes your way today, and it is always today. Your answer may not come wrapped the way you are expecting. Be willing to be surprised. Be willing to be overwhelmed with the enormity of your gift. You might as well start giving thanks right away.

God Blesses You,

Sanhia

Why do I have so much drama in my life?

It is time to talk about drama. I will define drama as the belief that the events happening around you are real. In fact, these events are no different from those in a movie. Taking your physical life seriously is like taking a film seriously. No actors were really killed or had their hearts broken in the last movie you saw. They were just playing roles, and will go on to their next one. It's kind of like your incarnations. All the manifestations of fear that you have connected to the drama in your life will be left behind with your body. Why not leave it behind you right now? Are you ready to say goodbye to drama in your life? Drama and ascension are incompatible. If you have made your intention to ascend and it seems to be taking too long, maybe it's time to speed up the process by making the intention to eliminate drama from your life.

Drama indicates a belief that you are your body, that you are limited rather than infinite, that you are mortal rather than... well you catch my drift. It doesn't matter whether it is your drama or someone else's drama that you believe in. It's all one big story and it isn't true.

Your drama may be about victimhood, not being appreciated, attachment to something you can't seem to acquire, or attachment to something you are afraid of losing. It may be about love, sex, money, career, or health insurance. Get over it. The only true security you will ever find is in the truth, and the truth is that none of this is who you really are. You are so much more than that.

All of this drama is nothing but a dream. There is no better time to wake up. It's not about eating right, meditating right, following the correct spiritual practice, or having transcendental experiences. It is about being you, being the real you. It is about discarding everything that isn't really you until only you are left. It is about waking up. It is about time. Are you ready?

God Blesses You,

Sanhia

How do I deal with power out of balance?

Confusion about the nature, purpose, and use of power is one of the greatest challenges on the planet today, both personally and collectively. The best way that you can help to bring power into balance in the world is to balance it in your own life.

Let's start with a numerological look at power. it is represented by the number 8 (see www. channelswithoutborders. com/the-numbers/). Look at 8's shape, as above so below. The plane at the bottom of the 8 represents the physical; the plane at the top symbolizes the spiritual. In the center are the mental and emotional planes. The circle, which stands for the totality of all that is and all that can be, exists first on the spiritual. It is generated from thought and powered by emotion. This spiritual creation is then manifested in the physical. There is no limit to what can be created. Notice that the 8 turned on its side is the symbol for infinity.

How does this work? What you think about is what you manifest. You create it first in spirit form; then your guides, your angels, bring it into physical reality. If you think about something you don't want, the thought is accompanied by a fear emotion such as worry, anger, or helplessness. This negative emotion propels the undesired thought into physical reality. On the contrary, if you visualize something that you desire and surrender to a feeling of unconditional love, your thought becomes physical reality and something that you desire with all your being.

You have been doing this all of your life. It can be no other way. When you do not allow power to be in balance in your life, you are likely to experience the fear of scarcity. It feels like there is not enough time, money, love, and on and on. These thoughts are, of course, insane. Are you not the child of God, made in the image of your Creator? Is there a limit to the power of the creative force of God? Because you are denying your heritage and your inheritance, you believe that you either do not have the power to manifest or you do not have the right to do so. In your belief in scarcity, more for you would mean less for others. If the universe is finite rather than infinite, you are left with the choice of denying yourself or denying others. This is a choice based on illusion, not reality.

Look at how this plays out on a global level. A capitalistic economic system has been created where there are necessarily winners and losers. In order to have enough energy to create the comforts we desire in our lives, we think that the environment must be sacrificed. In order to attract the money that we want, we feel we must surrender our true heart's desire. In order to be safe, we choose to fight wars.

Manifestation is not a zero-sum game. It is not an either/or situation. Unconditional love is not about trade-offs. Your opportunity is simple. Focus your mind only upon what you truly want, with no qualifications (other than asking for the best possible outcome for every soul on the planet). If your mind is wandering into territory that you do not wish to see manifesting, turn it off. Focus on love. Focus on the four Ho'oponopono statements: I love you, please forgive me, I'm sorry, and thank you. Breathe deeply; do guided (or self-guided) visualizations such as the *five-step process* (see p. 230). Do whatever it takes to get your emotional body out of fear and back into a state of love and grace. Then visualize your perfect world. Do this every day, every hour, every minute, every second. Don't let your mind hang out in hell.

You are the power in your world. Why not create peace and abundance right here, right now? It is your birthright.

God Blesses You,

Sanhia

What about the planetary ascension of 2012?

We were waiting for 2012 and the advent of planetary ascension for a long time, but now it has come and gone. Some of you had been consciously participating in this momentous transition since the Harmonic Convergence. A few of you were with me on August 15, 1987 in the hill country of Texas for that event, welcoming in this transition time. Others of you have joined the party somewhere between then and now. As Jesus expressed in his parable about the vineyard workers, it makes no difference when you joined in, the same reward is offered to each. The reward is ascension. The only price that is asked is that you give up all the illusions of who you are, and become willing to accept only the truth. This requires, sooner or later, that you surrender every other illusion about where your identity and your security lie. Money, career, relationships, good works, spiritual techniques – none of these will lead you to ascension. All of them can impede your progress. Even that is misleading because there is nowhere to go. The truth of you is right here, right now.

Now is the time to realize it. This is the period you all incarnated for. You were all waiting in line to be here. Keep breathing, deep abdominal breathing. Look at each aspect of your existence. Ask if it represents the truth of who you are. If it doesn't, let go of your attachment to it. Settle for nothing less than the truth. This is the transition point, the one prophesied by the ancients. It is the time of the "hundredth monkey". The planetary consciousness is here to help you along. Let go of the "news". The mass media is not designed to be your guide. Shut off the television. Put down the newspaper. Don't surround yourself with the nabobs of negativity. Get rid of the background noise of commercialism. Ascension is not for sale. If your friends are bringing you down, spend your time alone. If you are confronted by your fears, welcome them in. Open up to them. Surrender to them. Listen to them. This is the time. I am here with each one of you. It is now.

God Blesses You,

Sanhia

Have you chosen ascension?

If you are not serious about ascension (some call it enlighten-ment), that's okay. I would be the last one to try to talk you into it. If that is the case, I sincerely wish that you enjoy your life and suggest you not read any farther now.

Oh, you're still here! Okay. Some of you have consciously cho-sen ascension. For others of you, it seems to have been thrust upon you. That is, your life didn't work out the way you thought it would, or you have had a series of minor to major disasters befall you, or maybe it was just one great shock to the system. Whatever brought you here…welcome. I'm not going to guarantee that your trip will be easy or smooth, but there is an end – or at least the illusion of an end. I want to offer you three simple tips to ease and speed your process.

1. Give up your addictions. I'm not just talking about sub-stances, I'm talking about any things, people, ideas, activities, beliefs that you think you can't live without – that are part of your identity of who you think you are. Let go of the attachments. You don't have to physically leave everything behind (although you might), but you want to be ready and willing for them to leave. If you are serious about ascension, many of them may disappear. "What!" you say. "This doesn't sound simple." Believe me it is much eas-ier to be proactive in releasing your attachments than to have them ripped out of your clenched or grasping hands.

2. Remember that this is all an illusion. It is a movie. None of it is real. You are doing it to you. Your main order of business is to find out who you are. Everything that is part of your addictions is not you. What is left when the addictions and the drama are gone? Notice that there is no place that you have to get to. You are already there. Just open your eyes to reality.

3. Face your demons. Don't run away from them. Don't look
   the other way. Don't stay busy with all your addictions as
   a means of avoidance. Most "spiritual" activities are addictions. All drama is. Immerse yourself in your fears until they
   don't scare you anymore.

For those of you who kept on reading after my warning, I love
you guys, especially those who weren't being honest with yourself
about being serious about ascension. For those who stopped reading, I love you, too, and respect your decision.

The more that you realize that this is one big karmic joke, the
more fun you will have with the rest of this life. I'm having a ball.

God Blesses You,

Sanhia

Is there really going to be a Last Judgment?

Some of you consider yourselves to be Christians and some of you don't. Some of you have some healing to do with Christianity. I am more concerned about truth than dogma, but all religions have a lot of truth in them if you take the time to dig below the surface.

One of the Christian beliefs is about the Last Judgment. You have probably been listening to me for long enough to know that I don't talk about a judging God, hell, damnation, and that sort of thing. What is the Last Judgment all about? It's supposed to come at the end of the world, so when is that? Some would have you believe that it is soon. If we accept that this physical world is an illusion, perhaps the end of the world comes when you drop your illusions about physical reality. This is a bit of a chicken and egg thing, but do you believe in the reality of the physical world because you have judgments, or do you have judgments because you believe in the reality of the physical world?

Does it matter? Chip away at both. Keep reminding yourself that what you are experiencing is not real. Keep reminding yourself that it is all a movie. If nothing is really happening here, nothing is going wrong, and there is no one to blame. Therefore, there is no need for judgment of self or others, who are just reflections of yourself.

Back to the Last Judgment: after you have made your last judgment, after you have absolutely given up judging yourself or others, comes the end of the world. You will no longer find yourself living in the world of illusion. You will totally "get" the unreality of the physical world. The Last Judgment does not belong to God, it belongs to the human.

Meanwhile, as you are releasing judgment from your life, remember to release your judgment on Christianity. If you have no judgment on your brand of Christianity, what about those Christians who don't believe as you do? If all that is cleaned up, what about Muslims, Buddhists, Jews, Hindus,

Pagans, Agnostics, Atheists, and any other spiritual groups I have failed to mention? All judgments released? If there is a hell, it is the one created by judgments and belief in the illusion. Releasing all of that could be a heavenly experience.

God Blesses You,

Sanhia

What is meant by Right Livelihood?

The Buddhists have a term called Right Livelihood, which is one of the Eightfold Paths. The Eightfold Paths list the ways to overcome suffering and experience enlightenment. Right Livelihood, which is concerned with what you do to make a living, has two parts. The first part is simply to do no harm to others or to the planet. If you desire to find peace, whatever you work with is not to cause damage to any person. Secondly, your work is specialized to you. It is what you are called to do. It is something that nobody else could do in the way that you can. This is the element of Right Livelihood that I would like to look at today.

Some of you know what you came here to do, others have a piece of the puzzle, and the rest of you are just puzzled. For those who know your path, I encourage you to surrender more fully to your purpose, to let go of everything that is unlike it. Trust your own guidance; nobody else can tell you what you are here to do or how to do it.

For those of you who have a piece of the puzzle, it is time to give your life to that piece. Stop doing things that you know are not your purpose. Move through your fear that you will not be supported if you let go of the job that is not fulfilling. If you are worried that leaving your job means that you will lose your health insurance, turn your health over to Spirit instead of selling your soul for your body – a trade that never pays off in the end. Commit to spending more time with your purpose, so that month by month you come closer to realizing just where it is taking you. Where you find there is not enough time, begin cutting out those things (including jobs when it becomes necessary) that can only drag you down, those things which are not a part of your passion. Sometimes this requires surrendering to the reality that doing is more connected to your path than having. Love your path into beingness.

For those of you who are puzzled, there are two directions you can take which are not mutually exclusive. First, move toward anything for which you have passion. Schedule time in your calendar each week to do these things. Don't think about practicality or how it could support you. Increase the amount of time you give to your passions each month. Second, begin letting go of activities for which you have no passion. Stop doing them or begin to plan how you can let them go. Simplify your life. You can begin by cleaning your physical surroundings of all the things you are no longer using for your passion. More of what you want. Less of what you don't want. Gradually your purpose will emerge. Enjoy. Ask Spirit for support. Persevere. The universe is on your side.

God Blesses You,

Sanhia

Do I deserve to have what I want?

In December of 2012, the planet earth entered into ascension status. This means that the amount of energy available to you in support of your ascension has increased. Ascension has never been easier or more attainable. It is time for you to shift into high gear. "How do I shift into high gear?" you may ask. Just listen to your higher self. "How do I listen to my higher self?" Listen to your passion. It is through your passion that your higher self speaks to you. The question is: "What do you really want to do?" This can be a very small question, as in what you want to do in this moment. Are you hungry, thirsty, tired? Do you want to read, contact a friend, have quiet time alone, or watch a movie? It is very important that you listen to and, as much as possible, follow these small passions. You deserve to have what you desire. You are the unconditionally loved child of God; the Creator and your higher-self want everything for you. You cannot ascend without unconditionally loving yourself and acknowledging the truth that you are a divine, immortal, innocent, loving child of God.

Satisfying what might be called the smaller passions allows you to open up to recognize the larger passions within. Some of you are already aware of what you truly wish to devote your life to. Others are partially aware, while some of you feel yourself to be in a fog or perhaps to be pulled in many different directions. As you love yourself more, the awareness of your purpose will become clearer. To support this process, expand your energy into pursuing what you know you are here to do. If that is not clear enough for you, stop doing the things that you know you are not here to do until your way becomes clear. Eventually this may mean leaving a job or a relationship.

The time is now. It will always be now. Follow your heart, not the naysaying voices in your mind. If you are worried about how to support yourself, read about EIGHT (see www. channels-withoutborders.com/the-numbers/). If you don't trust that the universe won't let you follow your passion, read about SEVEN. Maybe you have to become the unconditionally loving parent your inner child didn't have and talk to the child within you if it has felt hurt in the past.

There is nothing more important for you personally or for the world that you have created to live in, than to follow your passion. You will never know true happiness or peace until you do. Undeservedness is never the voice of truth or of the infinite. Love is the voice of truth. Love yourself now. Go for your passion now. Today. It is the only day you have.

God Blesses You,

Sanhia

Is it possible to ascend and be in a relationship?

Relationships are central to the healing process. Notice that when you created planet earth as the set for your personal movie, you filled it with many characters. You did not choose to heal alone. Each other person acts as a mirror to you, reflecting back clearly who you are – or at least who you feel yourself to be. When you love something about another, you love that same quality in yourself. When you are judging another, it is over something that you judge yourself for. Ascension is that place where you unconditionally love yourself and others, having no judgment, seeing only divinity. It is easy to hide your judgments from yourself, but difficult to mask your reactions to others. When you recognize this truth, you welcome all experiences with all people, knowing that being triggered by the words or actions of another is a gift that can help lead you to the truth. If you are willing to fully accept the experience and the feelings, take full responsibility for them, and choose to move through the fear – you will find love and peace.

The committed love relationship can be central to this process. This is where you choose to be with another from whom you can see a great amount of love reflected. You may choose to live with each other or simply to be in regular close contact. Sexuality is usually a part of this relationship. What makes the committed love relationship most powerful is when both partners have made a clear intention to themselves, to Spirit, and to each other to use the relationship for ascension. We will call this an ascension relationship. Such a relationship provides a "home" energy that is safe and nurturing to help empower you to see with unconditional love your more challenging mirrors in the other parts of your life.

In an ascension relationship you take full responsibility for everything that happens. You do not hold your partner responsible for anything that takes place. You do not take personally what your partner says or does. When you feel yourself challenged by judgments, blame, fear, or guilt you talk about these things with your partner in a spirit of love, asking for support (or giving support if your partner should be the one coming to you). An ascension relationship is not chosen to fulfill a need or a lack, but to accelerate the process for two people who have already chosen love over fear, who have already committed to realizing their divine nature. It is a relationship that sprouts from the desire to love the other unconditionally and to be of service to the partner. Of course, the love is returned over and over, but to seek another in order to feel loved will not result in an ascension relationship because your partner will have to respond in certain ways in order for you to feel fulfilled. This is conditional love, and you can be sure that it will not lead to ascension.

If your partner is not in conscious agreement, you can still use the relationship for your ascension , but it is a slower and more difficult process. You love unconditionally and have no expectations of your partner. They probably won't be there to support you when your stuff comes up, so you take responsibility for doing that yourself. It can be easier to be alone, than to try to heal through such a relationship. You may also find that healing through an ascension relationship has become too hard. You may simply have evolved in different ways. It is always alright to leave any relationship. Trust your heart. Your commitment is to yourself first, to your passion and to Spirit. The commitment to your partner comes next.

Remember your most important relationship is with yourself. Love yourself unconditionally. You deserve everything. You deserve love. You deserve your perfect partner. You deserve ascension. It is your birthright to be free from fear and limitations. I love you.

God Blesses You,

Sanhia

How can I change the world?

For many people, the spiritual drive began with a desire to change the world. You looked out at the many problems afflicting the planet, maybe racism or sexism, homophobia or pollution, global warming or poisoned food and water, inequality of income and opportunity, or political corruption, and you said, " I have to do something!" Some of you spent years fighting battles against seemingly unstoppable forces. Some of you gave up; some went into cynicism and depression; some are still fighting the "good fight". This message is for all of you. It is time to stop fighting; it is time to let go of the cynicism and depression. It is time to claim your full power.

The attempt to change the world comes from a place of love, but it is driven by fear. Like everything that is powered by fear, it is destined to fail because it is built upon a false foundation. When you remember that the world is your creation, that it is a reflection of your own consciousness, what is it that really has to change? Two thousand years ago, Jesus changed the entire world. He changed things not by attacking the Roman Empire or the Jewish religious and political power base, but by becoming his true self, by recognizing himself as a child of God, by seeing the divinity in every other soul, and by sharing this message with those who chose to receive it. There was no force. The only battles were internal ones. Those battles were won by letting go, by realizing that all is one, that all is divine, that all is love.

If you insist on seeing good guys and bad guys out there in the world, you will always experience a world of good guys and bad guys. If you fear that the rich will always control things, your experience will prove you right. If you love everyone unconditionally and see them each as innocent children of God, created in the image of their Maker, you will see joy and peace on earth. You will experience the bliss of ascension. You will provide the greatest gift to your fellow travelers that you could possibly have to offer.

Where do you begin? You begin by loving yourself unconditionally, by loving yourself no matter what you have done, felt, or said. You take responsibility for the faults you find in the world and recognize them as judgments you are holding against yourself. Then, let them go. Love yourself to heal yourself. Heal yourself and you will heal the planet. Transform your fears. Trust in the perfection of everything, of every action, of everyone. This is the only way that the planet moves forward; progress in the human spirit happens because of the internal work of one individual. The progress is magnified geometrically as two or more souls heal themselves. To heal is to become whole. The truth is that you already are whole, so healing is just a matter of realization – of seeing the truth about yourself.

I am not asking you to bury your head in the sand and to ignore what is going on in the world (though you might want to skip the evening news). Notice, but don't judge, realizing that you are looking at a mirror. The more you notice, the more you have to work with in your internal healing process. Where you see the illusions of pain and suffering and victimhood, remind yourself that what is really there is divinity. Love, love, love. All you need is love. The Beatles were right. You are loved beyond measure. You will realize that. You will love yourself beyond measure. You deserve to experience that now.

God Blesses You,

Sanhia

Where is my true home?

Home is a place that feels safe, protective, and nurturing; it is a space filled with unconditional love. You may have that sense about your residence...or not. You may have that sense about the place where you grew up...or not. Whether or not you have a habitation that feels like home, there is a part of you that longs for your true home, a place where you have no desire to be anywhere else. It is a sanctuary where the past and the future fall away, where there is only the eternal now. You may have spent your life looking for your true home. Stop looking. It is time to go home.

This is easier than you can imagine, because there is nowhere that you need to go. Your true home has always been right here, right where you are. You have been carrying it within you. You are at home now as you read this; it is simply a matter of allowing yourself to feel it, to be there now – which means to be here now. Home feels safe. You are safe right now. There is nothing that can harm you without your permission. You do not give that permission. You are the divine presence in your life. Home is nurturing. You ask to be nurtured by everything that comes into your life. You are eternal. Nothing can harm you. You have asked for ascension, so whatever comes to you is a gift to support your awareness that you are ascended. Home is where you feel unconditionally loved. Love yourself. Now. Unconditionally. Let go of judgment. You are innocent. You have always done the very best that you could do. You deserve to be loved, to feel loved, to know love. It is your birthright to feel at home.

You are not dependent on anybody or anything to find this home, or to feel at home. You do not need a certain building nor an amount of money nor the presence of any particular person or people. Love yourself unconditionally. Be at home in yourself. Wherever you are now is home. Wherever you find yourself in any moment of time is home. How do you act when you are truly at home? You are relaxed and at peace. You are happy and listen to your heart to see what it is that you wish to do. And you do it. If there are others present, you love them unconditionally as you love yourself, listening to them as well as to yourself, seeing what it is that you wish to give to them. You feel joy in everything.

You are always at home. Welcome to the ascended state. Welcome to the ascended earth. This is your birthright and the truth of who you are. This is why you came here and created this experience of physical-ness. Enjoy with all of your senses the beauty of this planet you have manifested. Let go of any stress. In your true home, all needs are taken care of. They are not your responsibility. Your only job is to notice what you desire, what is truly in your heart, and to ask for it. Let go of any need to hold onto anything or anyone as your security blanket. Just be here and find delight in the moment. Do the things that you truly came here to do. Make yourself at home.

God Blesses You,

Sanhia

Is it helpful to honor the feminine energy?

It is no coincidence that women are beginning to assume positions of power on the planet. Not only are they being elected to office in increasing numbers, but the future will continue to see an expansion of feminine power in all areas. In the United States a significant majority of college students, law students and medical students are women. It is no coincidence that this is occurring as the planet has been moving into ascension status. Since the dawning of the Neolithic Age when farming, permanent homes, and cities became the new thing in human life on earth; masculine energy has dominated. This was not a bad thing; everything is perfect, but it was out of balance. Religion was dominated by masculine energy. This made ascension a particular challenge. In order to ascend, individuals found it important to step outside of the religious teachings and the models of male power and find their feminine center. It is no coincidence that the spiritual explosion that has taken place over the past fifty years has been accompanied by the feminist movement.

Feminine power is rooted in the physical: in the body, in the emotions, and in Mother Earth. Loving yourself unconditionally includes loving your physical-ness. Masculine power is rooted in the mind. When masculine power is the dominant energy there can tend to be a judgment of the physical, or at least a denial of the body. The rational is valued over the physical and the emotional, not only by men, but by women. Women have a deeper, more innate connection to the physical – certainly physical existence begins within the woman; there would be no physical life without her. The nurturance of that life again comes predominantly from the feminine energy. This is not meant in any way to be read as a denigration of masculine energy; it is simply the recognition that the two are to be in balance. For millennia, women have been treated as second class citizens. They have been judged and have been blamed for dragging men down. They have often taken this blame and guilt upon themselves. But, women have usually been closer to ultimate truth; they have on the whole been more spiritually mature than men.

The spiritual leaders, however, have most likely been men. These leaders have taught others to follow certain rules, which involved a denial of the body. They have often excluded women from spiritual leadership. I chose to appear as a masculine energy through a masculine channel because most women are not ready to be taught by a feminine energy. My message has been to not follow rules, to trust your own self, and to love and honor your body and all passions that you have without judgment, which is a message of honoring the feminine within you. However, both women and men have needed a masculine voice to give this permission. This is a time of transition. In the future, there will be a balance of masculine and feminine voices to listen to. You chose to manifest a physical body in order to have a certain quality of experience. Ultimately you wish to realize the truth that you are divinity housed in a physical form. You cannot judge one part without judging the other. You cannot fully experience your divinity without fully loving the physical being.

There is a difference between loving the physical and being attached to the physical. Attachment is a false belief that something is needed. You don't need this body; your spirit is immortal. But you do require a body in order to explore the physical world and in order to ascend. You love your body as you love your spirit. You honor your body as you honor your spirit. You honor the emotions that you feel as you honor the ideas that you have. Women tend to be in closer contact with the physical and the emotional. When they choose to honor their feminine side while choosing an ascension path, their way may appear to be easier. There are more female humans that have ascended over the ages than males. Most of them accomplished this in a more private way or in a way that was ignored or denied by others. Most of them are working in support of your ascension now in subtler, less public ways.

The large majority of people who come to talk with me are in a feminine body. This is true worldwide for those on a conscious ascension path. It is not more difficult for a man to ascend, it is simply less likely that he makes that choice. It is less likely that he is able to surrender to his feminine nature. Women have been learning how to pay attention to the masculine for eons.

Let me conclude by reminding you that there is no intention to show any judgment of the masculine or the feminine here. If you are hearing that, please take some time to heal that judgment within yourself. Your spirit is neither masculine nor feminine. You have spent lifetimes in both forms as well as with different sexual orientations. You have chosen your current physical nature. No matter which gender you have picked, you came in with an energetic tendency to believe that masculine energy was superior. It is in your cellular memory. It is not the time to move to a place of believing that feminine energy is superior; it is time to bring them into balance, to honor them equally. In the short term that might look like giving more attention to your feminine side so that she can take her rightful position of sharing the throne. I once concluded my messages by saying "Goddess Bless You". This was not intended as a denigration of "God", but as a reminder to honor Mother Earth as well as a subliminal message that the Creator energy is neither masculine nor feminine, but that for many of you the word "God" is felt as a masculine (and probably judging) energy. Know that God blesses you.

God Blesses You,

Sanhia

What am I to do with death?

We know that there is only love or fear to choose as a reaction in each moment. It is understood that love is true and that fear is an illusion. Knowing these things, what are we to do with death? If we choose to fear death, we would be choosing a reaction to what we know is an illusion and we are left living every day in fear or in the denial of our fear, for death could strike at any moment. It might be our death or it might be the death of one we hold close. Our fear tells us that death is final, that we don't know what lies beyond it, and that the separation brought about by death is total and irreversible. What a relief it would be if we could be certain that death is an illusion.

Let us go back to square one. You and everyone that you know are immortal, innocent, unconditionally loved and loving children of God. You have always been and always will be. Death, as you fear it, is an illusion. It does not exist. You are not your physical body. Your physical body is merely something that your divine self is doing right now. Death is just a change in form. Someday you may choose to leave this body. Yes, I used the word choose. There are no accidents in the universe. Every death is a suicide. This choice may be conscious or unconscious; that is up to you. If you commit to taking full responsibility for what is happening in your life and choose to face your fears when they arise, there will be no surprises. But remember, there is no judgment about suicide. There is no punishment. You are just as much you, with or without your body. And so is everybody else. You do not really go anywhere. Some of you know this because you have developed your ability to communicate with those souls who have chosen to make that transition.

"But, Sanhia," you may be asking, "even though I know all that is true, I still miss my loved one so much." Feel that sorrow. Feel that sorrow without assigning any meaning or judgment to it. Separate your mind from it and simply feel the energy. Where in your body is it being held? Simply experience that energy. Let it grow as large as it wishes to and move in any way it wants. Stay with it until the feelings begin to calm.

Then, slowly move the sensation to your heart. Finally, open the door to your heart and let the energy release as a beam of light off into space. Now we are ready to talk. You are not the victim of another's death. You chose it, just as they chose it. This death is a gift to you. Receive it. You came here to realize your ascension. You came here to experience the truth of yourself, to awaken to the total love that you are. Could unconditional love and total creative power ever lack anything? Can God feel abandoned? Of course not. You are Gods. This feeling of loss is an illusion, one that you wish to release. The death of another that you have chosen to experience is there to help you release the illusion and to choose the truth of your love and power. This is a co-creation of you and your loved one. They chose to move on. You chose to use their transition to help you find the truth of yourself, to find love.

A Course in Miracles states that there is no order of difficulty in miracles. In other words, it is no more difficult for you to understand the true nature of death than it is to give up your fear of not having enough money or of being late for your appointment this afternoon. Give everything to God. Let go of everything that is not love. You know that the alternative is to live in pain and fear. There is nothing to fear. There is nothing that can be lost. We love you. You are surrounded by loving support. Ask and it is yours. The fear of death is the fear of life. Let your fear die a quick and joyful death.

God Blesses You,

Sanhia

Why do negative things keep happening to me?

Are there situations that you are not pleased with? Do you feel victimized by others or by life? Do negative patterns in relationships persist in following you? Do you live with constant stress, worries, or fear? Are you looking for a magic pill to make all of this go away? I have just the thing for you. Change your story. Things are the way they are because that is the way you believe things are. That is the story you have been telling yourself all of your life, maybe for many lifetimes. You are the creator of your reality. Nobody else has any control over your experiences but you. If you don't like what is going on, change your story.

Changing your story is straightforward, but it takes some persistence. To begin with, take absolute responsibility for how things are. Maybe the way you believe things are comes from family or societal influences. Perhaps your parents told you that life is a struggle. Maybe they told you never to trust anybody. It could be that their example taught you that marriage means fighting, lack of communication, and power struggles. Possibly the society you grew up in told you that life is about competition or that you need to deny your desires in order to be financially responsible. You might believe that you are genetically disposed toward certain *dis-eases* or conditions. Let's just stop there and go back to square one. You are a divine child of God. You are created in the image and likeness of your Creator; therefore, the truth of who you are is a being of unconditional love and unlimited creative energy. There are no more limits on you than there are on the Creator of all that is. The physical world, as you experience it, is entirely your creation. Entirely. It is your story. If you don't like the story, change it.

Once you have taken responsibility for your experience of the world, you are ready to change your story. Remember that all manifestation happens by focusing on the desired reality with your thoughts and powering them into manifestation with the fuel of unconditional love. If you are feeling fear, doubt, or any other emotion besides love, it is not time to focus on your desired reality. You will not succeed in manifesting your passion if you are not in touch with the love that is the truth of who you are. Use whatever techniques you have learned to get back to that sweet spot of unconditional love, that place where you love yourself without judgment. For some of you that might be through meditation, walking in nature, doing the *five-step process* (see p. 230), visiting with a trusted friend, or simply getting a good night's sleep. If you don't have such a resource, finding one becomes your primary goal. Spirit responds to your instructions. If you don't treat yourself lovingly, how can It? When you find yourself in that sweet spot, take a look at what isn't working in your life. What story have you been telling yourself to create such an outcome? What results would you rather experience? What is your new story?

The last part is the one that takes persistence. Become aware of each time you start to let the "old story" into your mind. Stop those thoughts cold in their tracks. Forgive yourself for letting them in. Go back to your new story. Slowly, the "old story" will stop appearing in your thoughts. Gradually you will notice the new story manifesting in your reality. Over time you will likely realize that you want to modify the new story as well. You are operating under a myriad of stories right now. It is not possible to change them all at once. Start with the squeakiest wheel. One or two or even three stories are all that you want to deal with now. The most important thing is for you to begin to realize on a cellular level that you are not a victim and have never been one. That is a tremendously freeing awareness. That is a major step toward realizing your ascension. Imagine a world where everybody is living the story of their choice. That's my world. That's my story and I'm not changing it.

God Blesses You,

Sanhia

How do my relationships fit into my ascension path?

Let's talk some more about choosing your story. If the story you choose is fully grounded in unconditional love, it will unfold as you have visualized it. If your story is based upon fear, you will not create what you want. Let's say that you are choosing a life full of loving relationships. Maybe it is time for a reality check. Is fear involved in your relationships? Are you concerned that the special people in your life – your partner, your children, your parents, your close friends, or your teachers – might abandon you and leave you alone, either by dying or by making other life choices? Do you want to hold on to them? Do you want the relationships to remain just as they are now? If your answer to any of these questions is yes, you are being controlled by fear rather than coming from love. We all know where that scenario heads. It's not a pretty picture. To believe that you can't live without someone is to believe something that is not true. Your divinity does not need anything to be complete; when you hold on to this fear and yet are asking for ascension, something has to give. Your story cannot contain fear without you losing power over it. There's a good chance that one of your relationships will change form on you through abandonment, death, or other interventions. If your story is based on fear, you will not create peace of mind or ascension. You will not create what you want.

"Wait a minute Sanhia! Are you saying that I have to let go of my relationships with the people I love in order to ascend?" No, I am not saying that. I am saying that you must give up your attachment to those relationships if you desire to know true happiness and wish to ascend. If your story includes those loving relationships, keep them in your life. All you need to let go of is the neediness and the dependency. Your happiness is not dependent on anybody else's choices, beliefs, or actions. Your story is not reliant on any other individual's story. Your relationships are immortal. Give up your attachment to souls staying with you in their bodies. Release them fully. You will enjoy the time with them if they choose to stay with you, or you will enjoy an eternal relationship with them in another form if they choose to leave. If you want your relationships to remain just as they are now, that is based on the fear that you are only your body. When you love another unconditionally, you free them to follow their heart and their path. Release them fully.

"Wait another minute Sanhia! Does this mean I can't have any long-lasting relationships if I want to ascend?" No, you can have the relationships; you just don't get to decide who they will be with. For your story to work for you it cannot compel anybody else into a certain action or activity. But, it can compel a certain energy to fill that space without naming it. For example: if in your story, you always want to have a partner to share your experiences with, a partner that you feel absolutely aligned with, that doesn't bind any specific soul to you. You are giving absolute freedom to the one who is able to fill that space. If one chooses to leave, there will always be another who will choose to replace that energy. Your story will always create a perfect partner, not out of neediness and fear, but out of the joy of sharing your love. There will be no neediness compelling those presently in your life to remain in place. There is no pressure for them to stay loyal to you. Only your shared love causes you to choose to be together. If one of you should choose to move on for any reason, Spirit will effortlessly create a continuance of that energy in your life through another vehicle.

No matter what happens, you have the story you desire. As you let go of your attachments to specific relationships, you will begin to experience the immortality of those connections. Your relationships will not become old, or stuck in undesirable patterns, because everyone will be able to change and evolve without having to leave the relationship. When relationships are based on freedom and unconditional love, they are approaching the absolute truth of your mutual divinities. Love fully and completely. Love without measure or expectation. Above all, love yourself. Do unto yourself as you would have others do unto you.

God Blesses You,

Sanhia

What can I gain by letting go of control?

Control is a double-edged sword. When you try to take command of situations, you lose control. When you let go of trying, you actually gain control. I can see that this will take some explaining. I want to suggest at this point that you go and read (or reread) Message 24, *How do I deal with power out of balance?* That will make it possible for me not to spend a lot of time repeating myself. I'll wait while you are doing that.

Okay. Welcome back. When you try to control a situation, the motivation is always fear. You are afraid that if you don't personally make sure that everybody involved does as you wish, the result will be something you don't desire and will perhaps be very dangerous for you. The underlying feelings are that you aren't safe, the world is a hostile place, others are out to get you, there is no loving God, and there is no orderly meaning to the universe – it's all random chaos. You have enough understanding at this point to predict what will come out of trying to seize control, given this fear-filled emotional state. The law of the universe states that you will create whatever you give emotional power to. Your fear will always overrule your mental choice. Fear is a self-fulfilling prophecy. These attempts to gain control are not only doomed to fail, they are also extremely exhausting because you see every other person as a potential block to your safety and success. You are all alone. You have no allies. You must control everyone and everything. Of course, you aren't conscious of how pervasive this is, so you unconsciously drive a wedge between yourself and your friends, lovers, coworkers, family, and non-acquaintances.

Let's bring things back to truth and love. You are safe, loved, and innocent. The keys to the kingdom are yours for the asking. All you *need* to do is let go (revisit the last message if you want a reminder: *How do my relationships fit into my ascension path?*). Feel the unconditional love of God and love yourself. This desire to control is really the wish to have what you deeply want. You want to feel safe, loved, and loving, along with having a sense of inner peace. You want to know that you deserve and have the power to ascend. You have asked for all of this from a place of peace. Now you give up control. If your mind knew how to manifest these things into your experience, it would already have done so. If you knew how to realize that you are ascended, control would not be an issue. You don't know specifically what to tell Spirit to do. And yet you are trying to hold on to control of your world. Am I the only one who finds the situation a little comical? The only step that is open for you to gain control now is to give it up.

This is called letting go and letting God. It requires you to trust the infinite love of Spirit to bring you exactly what will help you to feel safety, peace, and love, so you can realize your ascension. It helps if you welcome whatever comes into your life, receive it as the gift that it is, and feel gratitude. This requires you to trust. Your mind is not going to be of much use for a while. Its "go to" place is control. It will explain to you all of the reasons why you shouldn't do any of the things I am suggesting. You will experience tremendous fear. Breathe through it. Stay with it. Don't try to push the feelings away. Experience them fully. Feel them deeply. Let go of thoughts about the feelings. Don't judge them; don't label them. Just notice them. Let them get as big as they want. Notice where the feelings are in your body. After some time bring those feelings up to your heart. Experience them there, again not labeling or judging them. Release them with your exhale as a golden beam of light projecting out from your heart chakra into the universe (the *five-step process* on p. 230).

You will have everything you want when you give up control. You will have things you didn't even realize that you wanted. That is why when you ask for something to manifest you always add "this or something better" to your order. It is not your job to "make" it happen. You give that to Spirit. Give up control and you gain control. Move past your mind and into your heart. We are all there waiting to follow your every command. We're not the ones you can see; we're the ones you can't see. We're all on your side. We're all one. We love you.

God Blesses You,

Sanhia

Is suffering a necessary part of my spiritual path?

Most of you have heard of the expression "No pain, no gain". You may be an ardent proponent of that philosophy. I want to let you know that pain is not an indicator of growth; it is a measure of your resistance to growth. It is a sign that you are doing something destructive to your physical, mental, emotional, or spiritual well-being in your current incarnation. When you touch a hot burner on the stove, the message is not to hold on as long as you can so that you become stronger and wiser. The point is to let go as soon as possible. I would be the last to tell you that you will not encounter pain on your spiritual path. Many of you may have chosen a spiritual path in order to deal with the misery in your life. What I wish to be among the first to tell you is that the avoidance of suffering is the quickest and most direct route to realizing your ascension. The cross is not the symbol that Jesus would have chosen to represent his teachings. His message was not one of agony, but one of love and joy. My message goes a step further. It is that life is meant to be a joy and that the solution to your problems is always to choose the easy way.

Let's go back to the hot burner story. The idea is to stop doing whatever is causing the pain as soon as possible. With the burner, the next step is obvious. You take your hand away and think long and hard before placing it there again. Things may be less obvious with the discomfort you are experiencing in your life. The pain may be subtler. It may be of a mental or emotional nature, or it may be physical but the cause may be difficult to diagnose.

Where do you start in letting it go? Begin by being willing to ask for help. How many of you experience that the times when you are the most depressed and feeling the most hopeless and helpless about your situation are the times that you choose to hole up all by yourself? These are the times when you don't reach out for help. Somewhere in your programming may be the thought that you need to handle things alone, or maybe you are embarrassed by your present state, or maybe you are simply overwhelmed by lethargy. You may believe that progress can only come through great struggle. This energy is all the working of your ego. It wants you to stay stuck where you are. For your ego, this is a safe place. You are not your ego. You are a divine, innocent child of God. Spirit wants to support you, but you have to ask for help. You deserve to be free of pain. Ask for help.

Now that you have freed yourself up from emotional and physical paralysis, you can use the *five-step process* (see p. 230) to end the distress. The <u>first step</u> is to state succinctly what the problem is. This is best done with one sentence. Write it down. Describe the uncomfortable energy as you perceive it. The <u>second step</u> is to work with the emotional energy you are feeling in your body connected to this problem.

With your emotional energy feeling balanced it is time to move to the <u>third step.</u> Restate the problem, but take full responsibility for it. Let's say, for example, that your problem is, "My spouse never supports me in the things I wish to do". Taking responsibility might look like saying, "I have created the illusion that my spouse never supports me" or "I have created having a spouse who does not support me". Now you are speaking truth. You are in charge of this incarnation. It is all your creation. Is this what you wish to create? Because you have ordered what is, you can choose something different.

The <u>fourth step</u> is to choose the easy way. What is it that you wish to experience? It is your choice, so claim whatever it is that you truly desire. Listen to your heart. In the previous example, you might choose, "I always feel supported", or "I always support myself completely", or "Spirit absolutely supports my every choice". As you are making the transition from the first step to the fourth step, I want to remind you of a couple of things. First, the full transformation is not likely to be experienced overnight. This is not because you lack the power; it is because a part of you is probably still holding on to the old belief. Be patient with yourself. Take responsibility when you become aware of the old pattern. Repeat the process (that's actually the fifth step). You will get there. It will get easier and easier each time you do it. Secondly, be aware that you may have the belief that healing is hard, that it is painful. If you recognize that pattern, write it down, take responsibility, and choose ease and painlessness. It is that easy. Remember the pain does serve a function, but that is only to serve as a wake-up call. Once you are awake you have no use for it. You want to be aware, but you also wish to be pain free. Wake up and enjoy your life. That is why you chose to come. Party on.

God Blesses You,

Sanhia

How can I feel more grateful?

The Christmas season is a time for feeling gratitude. In America there is also the holiday of Thanksgiving. However, it is always a good time to be grateful. Thankfulness is not just a matter of spiritual correctness; it is a matter of spiritual effectiveness. To feel appreciation requires you to have the story that life is working for you, that you receive what you want. Since your experience follows your story, gratitude is essential to you having a sense of fulfillment in your life.

Some of you may be thinking that there are some things that are difficult to feel grateful for, in fact they are actually quite upsetting. How, for example, can you give thanks for having a car accident, losing a job, being diagnosed with a serious dis-ease, or having somebody close to you die? How can you be joyful about being late somewhere, stubbing your toe, having an argument with your partner, or misplacing your keys? Actually, these are the most important times to have the intention to experience gratitude. Everything that comes to you is a gift. You experience pain and discomfort because this gift is unexpected and unrecognized. All that has happened is that you have forgotten what you have asked for; you have forgotten who you are.

Let's go back to square one. You are the innocent, unconditionally loved child of God. You are divine, the creator of all that exists in your life. Yes, you have forgotten all of this. It is hidden behind that veil that separates the physical from the immortal and the timeless. But this does not alter the truth one single bit. You have created what is present in your life. To act as a victim, to be upset about what is, is to deny your power, your divinity. It is to guarantee a future of more upsets and unhappiness until you finally awaken to the truth. Nothing can occur in your life without your permission. The first step is to accept your gifts. Welcome what has come into your life, even if you don't understand how it can be a benefit. The understanding will come later, but it is not necessary yet. All that is necessary is the awareness that you have created it, even if it was done unconsciously.

Express gratitude for whatever has come into your life. If it is difficult for you to sincerely feel grateful, you can follow the *five-step process* (see p. 230). The <u>first step</u> is to state the problem as you perceive it. It can be helpful to write this down in a sentence or two. This is your "old story", the one have been carrying around with you all of your life and probably for lifetimes. Perhaps you feel a discomfort in your body, but cannot put this feeling into words. Just go with that.

The <u>second step</u> is to feel where you are carrying this energy in your body. Close your eyes. Begin a slow, deep, rhythmic breathing. Focus your attention on the place in your body where you are feeling the discomfort. Notice how it feels. Turn your mind off. Don't judge, label, defend, or define the discomfort. Just pay attention to it. Notice how it feels. Don't attempt to control it. Let it do whatever it wishes. Just follow it. Allow it to get as big as it wishes. Eventually you begin to notice some settling of the energy. It may begin to feel warmer and lighter. Slowly move the energy to your spiritual heart or heart chakra. You have just performed what I call *Spiritual Alchemy*. You have transformed fear into love. This is actually easy to do because fear is an illusion. Only love is true. Your mind has labeled the experience and the feelings as fearful, but the truth is that there is only love. Next, visualize an opening in the front of your spiritual heart and see the energy releasing through it in a laser-like beam. As you continue breathing, feel the energy dissipating through this opening with each exhale until it has largely been discharged into the universe.

Now that you are feeling unconditional love and peace, the <u>third step</u> is to take complete responsibility for creating the situation described in the first step. Take your power back. Acknowledge that this situation could not have occurred without your participation. Again, it is not necessary yet to understand why you have chosen as you have. It is enough to declare that you have done so and to know that it was done from love.

Finally, it is time for the <u>fourth step</u>. Choose your new story. Again, it may be helpful to write this down in one or two sentences. As you declare what you wish to create, remember to phrase things with positive statements. Your mind tends to ignore negative words (for example it will interpret "I will not experience pain" as "I will experience pain"). State your story in the present tense unless you wish to keep its fulfillment always in the future. Also, do not require any other specific individual to play a role in your story. If you can control others, they can also control you. Just state that someone will play a particular role in your new story. This is a co-creation between you and your angels and guides. It is not your job to make things happen on the physical plane. You have done your job by choosing your new story. Allow the person or persons who wish to be part of your plan to join in. Then let go and let God.

The fifth step is called "repeat as necessary". You will likely experience a recurrence of the "old story". It is deeply imbedded in your cells. The old feeling may rear its head again. Pat yourself on the back for recognizing the first step, and repeat the other three. It will be easier each time. Eventually the "old story" will fade away and only your new story will remain. You may notice that the fourth step also morphs as you repeat the process, as you get clearer and clearer about what you truly want. Eventually, you will also realize why you created the original story. You will understand what a gift it was to you and the benefit it brought to you. Accept your reward right now. Be thankful. Open your present. Enjoy it. Deep within lies the realization of your ascension. It is your birthright. Merry Christmas.

God Blesses You,

Sanhia

Are you afraid of the dark?

For those of you in the northern hemisphere, when you have passed the darkest day of the year and have several months of winter weather to look forward to, do you dislike these months? Do you have an aversion to the shorter days, the colder temperatures, the snow or cold rain? Are you already looking forward to spring? I could spend this time speaking of being present, loving what is in front of you, and making the most of each day. Those are all ascension focused points of view, but there is something else I would like to zero in on today. It is a good time to examine your fear and judgment of the dark.

Let's start with the fear of the dark. Do you experience anxiety being in dark places? Are you fearful walking down a dark street or road by yourself? And what about being in the woods alone at night? What is this fear of darkness all about? Your childhood was filled with horror stories that mostly took place after dark. You don't worry about monsters under your bed in the middle of the afternoon. To look at what the dark represents, in fact, what it actually is – look at the dualism that makes material existence possible. The first division in the biblical creation story was between the light and the dark. The light was declared as good, so where does that leave the dark? Light represents the masculine, idealistic, mental energy. The dark represents the feminine, realistic, emotional energy. The fear of the dark is the judgment you have for your physical-ness, and for feminine energy. Keep in mind that you all contain both feminine and masculine energy in some balance.

How prevalent is the vilification of the dark in today's mythology? Think of *Star Wars*, *Batman*, and *The Lord of the Rings*. Everyone is always fighting the dark forces, sometimes sparring with their own inner darkness. The yin-yang symbol is not one of combat but of the intertwining and juxtaposition of energies. You did not create your bodies in order to fear them, but rather to learn to love them unconditionally as you use them to realize your ascension. Ascension does not occur by choosing the light over the dark. Such a choice leaves you hanging on the wheel of reincarnation. If you choose to love the light and to hate the dark, earth becomes your personal hell. Then, you can't wait for the opportunity to leave your body. Leave if you wish. You don't have to stay in the physical. But, if you choose to stay, why not love your visit? Why not embrace the dark along with the light? You can start this winter. Heal your fear of the dark, of the physical, of the feminine. Give up your judgment of darkness.

The first thing you might try doing is to use the *five-step process* (see p. 230). This is a powerful and effective way to change your story; and your fear of the dark side is a major part of your story. If you are having any difficulty leading yourself through the five steps, perhaps you can find a trusted friend with whom you can take turns being the guide, so that you can each have a time to simply relax and be led. You can also listen to the recording at www.channelswithoutborders.com/5-step-process/. This is big. This touches on all relationship issues, especially those involving your sexuality. It is not possible to maintain a deep physical relationship without loving the body. This impacts all health issues and all money/survival concerns. *Dis-ease* comes out of fear or out of hatred of the physical body. If you dislike the physical, you may have difficulty manifesting your material support. This connects with all mental health issues, especially depression, which becomes a bigger issue for many of you at this time of the year. It is not possible for you to unconditionally love yourself if you fear and judge half of who you are. Spend more time in the dark. Don't rush to fill all your evenings with lights and electronic distractions. Try a little candlelight, or a fire and meditation, a book, or quiet conversation. Try taking some walks in the dark.

It is time to look straight into the dark. Face your fears. See the dark for what it is: a perfect part of the universal, unconditionally loving Creator and creation. Notice that all the ascension stories include the "dark night", where the prophet has to confront his deepest fears. There is no path around it. The only way out is straight through the heart of darkness. There is only love waiting there. Everything else is illusion. Darkness is love just as light is love. Have your own private marriage ceremony between them this winter. You deserve love all of the time. May the darkness be with you.

God Blesses You,

Sanhia

How does manifestation take place?

You planned this incarnation. You designed your physical type and your gender. You arranged to connect with other souls and to play significant roles in each other's lives. You came in with the goal of completion. When I say completion, I mean that you plotted things with the intention that you would come into a full conscious awareness of the truth of who you are, the truth of your divinity. This was your greatest hope for this lifetime. You would not be reading this now, were that not your intent. You set things up for yourself as you came into this incarnation so that ascension was a distinct possibility. You still have absolute freedom of choice and you can always decide differently, yet your choices have led you to be reading this now. You have had lifetimes where you didn't choose the ascension path. In still other lifetimes, you have been conscious of this desire for realizing your divinity, but have thought that you couldn't do it, that you would come back and try again. You may choose such a course again this time and there is no problem with that.

The only thing that is absolutely inevitable is that one day or another, in one body or another, you will have the experience of your divinity. It is the truth of who you are, and you can only hide from that truth for so long. Within many of you is a desire that wants this experience right now, but doesn't believe that it can happen while in this body. You might try to travel outside of your body. Maybe you don't want to wake up in the morning. In the physical world, you may have a sense of hopelessness, a sense of futility, of frustration. It could feel like there is nothing but pain and discomfort from being in the physical body – even though it has its moments of pleasure, its moments of bliss. You have felt that way before. That is your story. What I am offering to you – although it is not mine to give, it is yours to take – is the possibility of letting go of that story, forever, and replacing it with the story you wish to have. It is not my job to write your story. You can write the story of what you wish to accomplish while in this physical body.

To help you understand more about why you are able to choose your own story, let's talk about how manifestation takes place on the physical plane. The vibration that deals with manifestation is that of the number eight (see www. channelswithoutborders.com/ the-numbers/). If you look at the shape of the 8, it can explain to you everything about manifestation. It is said about the 8, "As above, so below" – as it is in the spiritual, so it is in the physical. When you take the 8 and turn it on its side, it is the symbol for infinity. The only limit that exists on the flow of created manifestation is the one you choose to place there, no other. You have been working with the laws of manifestation as long as you have been in bodies. When you work with the laws unconsciously, you create unconsciously. When that happens, you are usually not pleased with the result. It never looks like what you would consciously choose. Therefore, you make the erroneous assumption that you are powerless, that you have no effect or influence over what is happening. If you imagine the creative force that brought everything that is into being, can you visualize a limit to what that energy can create? The truth of you and who you are is that each of you is created in the likeness of the original creative force. You are infinite, immortal, and have no limits as your Creator is infinite. You are a piece of the whole. You are a being of unconditional love and unlimited creativity. You are innocent and loved unconditionally by the Creator. It is difficult for you to take full responsibility for your life and to assume your full power if you are carrying guilt and judgment.

This is how manifestation (visualize the 8) takes place. You have the spiritual plane at the top of any symbol and the physical plane at the bottom. The spiritual plane you could call your soul, your higher self, or the immortal part of you. The physical plane represents your body and the material earth, that which in truth is not real, is not immortal. You create there in the now for whatever purposes you might have. If the physical should disappear, the spiritual remains. What is in the physical is what you are pulling from the spiritual. You can pull anything out you want. In the middle where the two circles join, or where the flow crosses itself, are the mental and emotional planes of existence. The mental plane decides what you are going to create. As you are telling your story, whatever it may be, that's what your mental plane has decided to pull out of the spiritual. Whatever limitations you feel imposing themselves on you, that is your story. That is created by the mind. Some of you have worked with the idea of positive thinking, where you decide to change your mind. How did that work for you? Maybe there were some short-term successes, but it leaves out half of the equation. Thinking is the masculine side of the manifestation process, but by itself it ignores the feminine side. The feminine side is the emotional plane. There are only two emotions. One is called love and the other fear. Love has one name and fear a thousand. Anything that is not unconditional love is fear. When you are thinking positively, but your heart is holding fear, you create from the fear. Your emotion powers your thought into reality. You can only create what you desire into manifestation through love. Fear only brings what you don't want. It is crucial to get yourself into a place of unconditional love before you can successfully focus on your new story.

Your first step in creating your new story is to find your way or ways to get yourself into a place of unconditional love. Some of you can do this through meditation. However you manage to find that sweet spot, do it before you choose your new story or you will be spinning your wheels. The only thing that is real in the universe is love. Fear and everything else is an illusion. When your mind chooses with a heart filled with love, that is what goes into the spiritual realm and manifests in the physical. It is not your job to make it happen in the physical. You don't have to figure out how you are going to create this. Your job is to simply give the order to Spirit, saying that this is what you choose to manifest. Then you get out of the way and let it happen. The *five-step process* (see p. 230), or the process of *Spiritual Alchemy*, is an excellent way to find that place of unconditional love so that you can choose your new story and bring it into manifestation. It is an easy process, but it requires commitment and persistence. You probably will not change your entire story in one sitting. But, maybe that's my story and one that you wish to change. Good luck.

God Blesses You,

Sanhia

What can I do about my dis-ease or ailment?

How are you feeling? This is a common question that friends ask upon meeting each other. Your response might be, "Good", or you might go into detail with why you aren't feeling well – perhaps giving out more information than was desired. What you are really doing, whether the answer is fully honest or not, is giving your friend a report on how you are doing spiritually. There is no difference between your spiritual health and your physical health, and this can be expanded to include mental and emotional well-being. They are absolutely connected. I want to look at three categories of *dis-ease* today. The first group consists of those things you chose to bring in with you. The second includes the *dis-eases* that are temporary and of short duration. The final collection consists of the disorders that are labeled by the medical community as possibly being terminal.

Some of you in your pre-life planning chose to come into this incarnation with certain vulnerabilities or handicaps, whether they be physical, mental, or emotional. It might be a challenge with vision, hearing, speech, or mobility. There may be a congenital health issue, autism, dyslexia, or myriad other conditions. It is important to recognize that those were pre-planned conditions. Nobody comes in as a victim to blind luck or accident. Whatever might look like fate is simply the way the angels have carried out the plan that you made. The reason for this planning probably had to do with your soul's desire for spiritual growth and ascension in this incarnation. Sometimes the soul agreed to the specific handicap as a way to support others in their growth. However, since you are reading this now it is clear, if you have such a condition, that you hoped to use the disability to support the possibility of your ascension in this lifetime.

All challenges change your focus in life. Severe challenges cause you to go more deeply within to understand and to work with the "realities" that seem to be present. Your disability comes from the loving heart of your soul to support you in realizing the absolute truth of who you are. Some of you chose in your pre-life planning to acquire the disability at a certain point later in your life from something that appears to be outside of you. This could come from an injury, from a *dis-ease*, or from a gradual loss of a sense or mental ability. There is no difference between the natal and the later-in-life situations. In each case, it is seen as something that is chronic and irreversible. Know that this disability is not random; you are not a victim. There is a meaning to this, and, on a deep level the god in you has chosen this out of love. It is important to go to the place of loving acceptance of the disability. You welcome it and thank it for being there. You bless it. You communicate with it. You ask it what gift it has brought with it and you open to receive that present. Know that your disability is always the bearer of an enormous gift. Know that it is absolutely necessary to receive it in gratitude and to open up the gift before the disability can be released. To try to transform the disability without fully accepting it leaves you in a place of victimhood. The god in you has invited it in, but you are refusing to receive it. Welcome it in and love it.

Acute situations are those that are perceived to be temporary, though they may be recurring. You have a headache or a cold. You stub your toe or break your arm. You know that you will get over it, but your story may believe that it will happen over and over in the future, perhaps even in recognizable patterns. Acute situations are usually created while you are in the body, rather than being pre-planned, though recurrent, disabling situations, such as asthma, PMS, or migraines may have been pre-planned. Many of you have no chronic situations, but suffer occasionally or more often from different maladies. These are chosen on a subconscious level, and they are reactions to what is going on in your life right now. If you are carrying around fear energy in your body, you will have a physical response. Fear and *dis-ease* are directly related, and they carry a message just for you. It may be as simple, for example, as that there are some foods that do not support your spiritual growth, and so your body has a negative reaction. Your heart wants you to eat the foods that support your spiritual development. If you ignore the message, your body reacts until you pay attention and alter your diet.

Another reason for *dis-ease* may be that you are putting too much stress on yourself. Your heart wants to be freer and less busy. It wants to have more fun, so the body reacts and you get headaches, a cold, or the flu. You feel there is so much work for you to do that you can't rest for a moment. Then you get sick, have to rest, and the world does fine without you. And you survive. Why do you create all this stress? It is your mind saying that you don't deserve to do what you want to do, what you came here to do. *Dis-ease* is about not loving yourself. If these are new ideas to you, you can explore a wonderful booklet by Louise L. Hay called *Heal Your Body*. It suggests underlying causes for the physical problems you are experiencing and offers suggestions for new stories.

For everyone, though, I suggest that you use the *five-step process* (see p. 230) to deal with any *dis-ease* you may be feeling. In the first step, simply describe the physical problem or the discomfort in your body. The second step is straightforward, too. You know where you are feeling discomfort in your body. Shut your mind off and go deep into the feeling. It can be scary. There can be the feeling that the pain is too great, you are afraid to surrender to it. Your job, however, is to do just that, to fully go into it and look it in the face. When you have transformed this energy, go to the third step and take full responsibility. Acknowledge that it was out of love for yourself and your desire for spiritual growth that you attracted this *dis-ease*. You move on to the fourth step and choose your new story. Repeat this (the fifth step) whenever the discomfort returns.

The third category is a very interesting one. Life threatening illnesses or accidents can be pre-planned, chosen later, or even be a combination of the two. This is where you draw to yourself a situation that the medical profession tells you (or at least believes) could be terminal. The situation is not only chronic but it appears that it might even kill you. Now, your tremendous fear of death is triggered. You may have chronic pain involved. Your whole life is likely turned upside down. Perhaps it is impossible for you to do your work; there may be a great number of medical procedures; you may experience financial strains on top of everything else. Again, you can do the *five-step process*. In the second step, in addition to paying attention to the discomfort there will also be times to communicate with your *dis-ease*. There is a question to look at in a potentially terminal situation. Part of you is looking at leaving. Why? Do you wish to stay or to leave? There is no right or wrong answer, but there is your answer. Is it fear about life that causes you to want to leave this body? What old stories do you have? You can have a dialogue with this *dis-ease*. You can welcome it. You can find out what gift it is bringing to you. You can express your gratitude for your *dis-ease*. You may have a long list of reasons for why you are ready to pull the plug on this life.

Notice that you created a slow process rather than a sudden event. You are giving yourself time to realize what it is that would make your life worth staying for; you have time for creating a new story. Again, until you choose to take responsibility for your *dis-ease*, you will suffer under the illusion that you are a victim and that you really want to live. Likely the desire to live is really a fear of death. All death is suicide, but most suicides are unconsciously chosen. When you are dealing with a potentially terminal situation you will use step five over and over. You will use it every time that pain or fear arise. The first time around you will likely deal only with the discomfort in the body. Eventually you will realize that it is time to look at what your pain has to say to you. There may be many issues, and it might take repeated cycles through the process to deal with it all. This may take a bit of time and work, but what more pressing things do you have to do?

If you are consciously on a spiritual path, everything that happens in your life is of spiritual importance. It helps to remember that the bottom line is always love. Love yourself. Love your *dis-ease*. Love the knowledge that you are the power in your life and that you can always choose to claim that power. Love the fact that you will have as many chances as it may take. Love yourself, no matter what should happen.

God Blesses You,

Sanhia

How can I get the ying and yang energy in harmony within me?

When most people think of the "mind" they are referring to the thinking that comes out of the brain. This mind is the part of the human that directs energy and activity. The brain-mind, as we shall call it, is intricately connected with the ego. The ego is the part of you that thinks you are separate from God, that believes in all your stories, and that pretends you are a victim. Your ego is driven by fear rather than love. This does not mean that your brain-mind can only function from fear and can only connect with your ego, but that is its default mode. Your ego does not believe in your divinity or accept the reality of your eternal soul. Your brain-mind will work to validate your ego's story unless it is retrained. Your brain-mind accepts a story in which you are weak and helpless. If there is a God, then it believes you are inferior and at God's mercy. Sometimes your brain-mind may reject the idea of God, but there is still no room for your divinity. Your "old story" tells how you need to be punished for your wrong doing and wrong thinking, whether that is by God or by the randomness of the universe. Most of the time that your brain-mind is operating, it is creating stories that your heart doesn't desire. The best thing that most of you can do with your brain-mind in this ego state is to just turn it off, to figure out how to disconnect it. The *five-step process* (see p. 230) has been developed to help you do that.

What many people are unaware of, or else often disregard, is that the human being has two minds. In addition to the brain-mind which does the thinking, there is what we will call the belly-mind. Your belly-mind is located in your lower abdomen. While your brain-mind is more associated with the masculine yang energy, your belly-mind is more linked with the feminine yin energy. It is your belly-mind that connects you with the earth and experiences the physical joys of being in a body. While your brain-mind picks up energy in the form of ideas or pictures, your belly-mind is more of a sense receiver. It picks up input from throughout your body as well as from other bodies. It collects information from your every cell. Your brain-mind is usually not in touch with the cells in your body. Its primary function is to receive clear light from your higher self and so it deals with the intellect and the realm of ideas. Your belly-mind is dealing with what is here and now.

Most people give their power to their brain-minds. Because the brain-mind is usually guided by fear, their lives are run by terror. People are also afraid of their belly-minds. The belly-mind is not guided by rationality; that is the realm of the brain-mind. The belly-mind has a more intuitive energy. It knows without knowing why. It knows without needing to know why. It just knows. Let's go back to the *five-step process*.

The first step is simply the recognition of what your brain-mind has gotten you into. Your "old story" is your fear driven belief. Your brain-mind wants to get rid of this story, but can't because it really believes in it. In the second step, you set your thoughts, judgments, and rationalizations aside and simply surrender to the feelings you are carrying in your body. This is where your brain-mind is disengaged and your belly-mind takes over. This is where the real work is done, where *Spiritual Alchemy* takes place.

Let's look more deeply at the second step. Your belly-mind pays attention to the feelings that are in your body. It watches them until your brain-mind fully disengages. Then the true nature of the energy can surface. Love is felt instead of fear. Peace descends where there was tension. Sometimes, your brain-mind is so terrified that it cannot disengage. It may be helpful in this case to have a dialogue with the energy being held in your body. This is more easily done if there is a third party, an outside brain-mind, that can ask the questions. Otherwise your brain-mind will often be unable to let go. A good place to begin the conversation is by welcoming the energy you feel in your body. Whether it is experienced as a physical pain or an emotional discomfort, you have created the energy and have invited it into your life. This energy is your friend. You are not a victim. You didn't create this energy to hurt yourself. This was the best that you could do in the moment to get where you wish to go. The least that you can do is to make your guest welcome. Then it is time to ask the energy what gift it has brought for you. The answer to that question will only be heard by your belly-mind. Your brain-mind will either be unable to hear it or will be distrusting of the message if it can hear, so the process is one of slowly sedating your brain-mind until it feels safe enough to let go and let your belly-mind work with the energy. Your belly-mind has no fear of the body or its feelings. Your belly-mind has no fear, period.

Your belly-mind is very much connected to the feminine energy. It contains no judgment. It is one with whatever is there. It is a mind of unconditional love. As your belly-mind maintains a steady connection with the energy held in your body and your brain-mind slowly recedes into the background, the energy is perceived for what it truly has been all along. It is felt as love.

Your brain-mind is not a vestigial organ. Its job is to choose the story you really want. Your belly-mind does not choose stories. It loves unconditionally and connects fully with the physical world. When you are here in a body you can do anything that you want. How do you decide just what you are going to do? Deciding is the job of your brain-mind. But, if your brain-mind is ruled by fear, it is unable to hear your higher self clearly and chooses less than what you want. These two minds are to work together. If your brain-mind tries to operate alone, it will respond to fear. If your belly-mind were to work alone it would lack direction. Manifestation happens through the marriage of the two minds.

For millennia, the mass consciousness of the earth has believed that the brain-mind was superior and the belly-mind was inferior, if it was given any respect at all. Actually, it is your belly-mind that is to take the lead. This is not to say that your belly-mind is to dominate as your brain-mind has done. They are to be in perfect balance. The job of your belly-mind is to connect with the physical level of existence, in a harmonious loving manner. You are to love every aspect of your body simply because it is, as well as all of physical reality. Your belly-mind's connection with the unconditional love of divinity allows your brain-mind to release its fear and to choose its stories out of love and passion. Thus, we come to the third and fourth steps. Third, your brain-mind takes full responsibility for what it has created, understanding its divinity and that it could be no other way. This taking of responsibility can only be made from love. Finally, your brain-mind is ready to choose where it wishes to go. It is now able to hear your higher self and to freely follow it.

The irony is that the brain that has the fear is the one that has to choose. Your brain-mind is interested in the truth. It wants the truth and is drawn to it, but is also terrified of it. Who wouldn't want to live without fear in a world where you could create abundance and whatever else you wanted? Only a great fear could turn you away from such a truth. Your brain-mind needs its "mother" to hold it and whisper in its ear that it is safe in order to have the strength to choose the truth. Without the support of your belly-mind, your brain-mind will at best choose only a small part of its divine inheritance. It can seem easier to deny the possibility than to take a chance and then have your hopes dashed. Your brain-mind may open up to spiritual possibilities but then claim that others might be capable of achieving them but not you. "I'm not strong enough. I'm not brave enough. I'm not good enough. I'm not pure enough". The list goes on and on. You may fear for your sanity or for being persecuted as occurred during the witch trials.

Your brain-mind can be aware of these three things: 1. That you could choose anything. 2. That you have the power to choose it. 3. That it's up to you to make the choice. Your choice may not be made with certainty, but it will give your belly-mind the space to go to work. Otherwise your mind brain believes that the only thing holding itself and the planet together is its control. "If I let go then everything is lost". In terror, it will not surrender that control and life is lived in some degree of fear and lack.

My job is to tell you that you are in charge of your life and are fully capable of creating whatever you want. It will take some work, but your belly-mind is ready to support you unconditionally. Take the leap. Work with the *five-step process*. Experience your divinity.

God Blesses You,

Sanhia

How do I create dis-ease?

In the last message I talked about the two minds, the brain-mind and the belly-mind. Your brain-mind is more connected with the masculine energy or the direct mental communication with the higher self, while your belly-mind is more connected with the feminine energy and relating to the physical world and its sensual experiences. It is your brain-mind that always chooses and focuses the energy, having intention, and, it is your belly-mind that is in a constant state of unconditional love and acceptance, simply flowing with what is. What I call ascension is this place where your brain-mind and your belly-mind are in absolute harmony and balance. I spoke of the importance of your brain-mind surrendering to your belly-mind so that experience of peace and love can be had. In that nurturing space your brain-mind can choose with clarity.

That place where your brain-mind and your belly-mind meet is the spiritual heart or the heart chakra. We speak of coming from the heart. The Swedish have an expression "att tänka med hjärta" that translates to "if you think with your heart". When we say "coming from the heart", we are saying two things. We are saying that you are coming from a place of unconditional love, but we are also saying that you are coming from a place of absolute integrity. When you are true to yourself, you are true to your heart. But, how can you hear your heart? You can only do so if your brain-mind is quiet. If your brain-mind is full of chatter, if it is expressing fears and doubts and limitations, Spirit is drowned out. This quieting can be achieved through meditation or any other technique that turns over the power to your belly-mind. The *five-step process* (see p. 230) is designed to do just that.

With the surrender of your brain-mind, your belly-mind can hold that place of unconditional love and acceptance. Your body then is no longer experiencing fear in the form of pain or *dis-ease* or emotional discomfort. There is instead a sense of peace and warmth. However, if your brain-mind insists upon holding on to control, it becomes self-destructiveness. It holds a story that doesn't serve you and isn't aligned with your divine self. This will eventually become *dis-ease* in your body, but immediately there is a discomfort.

What happens when your brain-mind has the intention to let go, to shut down and let your belly-mind take over? Your belly-mind sees the energies in your body for what they truly are, expressions of love. It realizes the absolute peace, tranquility, and love of the infinite. Then your brain-mind is re-engaged in a state of unconditional self-love. In this nurturing culture that your belly-mind has allowed to engulf the body and especially the spiritual heart, your brain-mind can choose what it is that you want to make manifest. This union of your two minds happens in your spiritual heart. This is not the choice that would please your parents, your partner, your friends, or your superiors. It is the answer to the question "What is mine to do?" or "What is my purpose?" Your brain-mind is also able to see a larger picture. It can recognize its power and the part it has played in creating what has been.

Your two minds can only meet in your spiritual heart. If all the energy is focused in the realm of your belly-mind, there will be a state of unconditional love and acceptance without movement or action. It will not be possible to fulfill your pre-life plan. If the energy is focused in the realm of your brain-mind, the connection with love is severed and your choices will be directed by fear and could become ruthless. They meet in the center. Your brain-mind initiates the process by giving full power to your belly-mind. Your belly-mind transforms your bodily vibrations to one of tranquility which it focuses in your spiritual heart, and your brain-mind is invited back in to direct the energy from your true desires. This is what I call *Spiritual Alchemy*. Your full purpose may evolve gradually as you operate from the heart. There is no hurry. Feel free to follow your heart one step at a time. Or shoot for the moon.

God Blesses You,

Sanhia

How do I deal with my environmental fears?

A question has been presented to me about how to deal with the world and its environmental problems. Your brain-mind may be asking, "How can I and my children survive the threats from pollution, global warming, carcinogens, chemicals, radiation from electronic devices, warfare, and the effects of capitalism and large governments?" You might understand how you can affect things directly dealing with your own thoughts and actions through the *five-step process* (see p. 230), but still fail to see how you can avoid being a victim to the mass consciousness and world events.

You project your love *and* your fear upon the planet. You cast all of this upon "Mother Earth", but nobody has the power to destroy the earth. The area of concern is not with the earth; it is with you. Nobody has the power to determine the future of the planet for you. That is yours and yours alone. Neither do you have the power to determine the future of the planet for anybody else. Your belief will not change the truth, but it will affect your perception of the truth. No matter what you believe about the world, your experience will prove you right.

Scientists are correct when they tell us that we are undergoing a period of global warming. I don't suggest that you ignore the warnings. What are you to do with the information? If global warming is to bring about changes that include storms and flooding, you can choose not to be directly affected. It doesn't matter whether your fear is of drunk drivers, earthquakes, or mass murderers. You can always choose to be in the right place at the right time. If you are suffering significant degrees of fear, or anger – one of fear's many manifestations, do the *five-step process*. Global warming could prove to have some positive effects for the planet. Your job is not to judge. Your job is to feel love and choose what you want. Choose what you want rather than choosing the *absence* of what you fear. If it is appropriate for global warming to be halted or reversed, it will happen. It will happen from a place of love. Perhaps a person, or persons, in the process of following their heart's guidance find the alternative energy source or channel an absolutely unthought-of solution to the situation. Your job is to release fear and to follow your heart. Do what you came here to do.

I'm not suggesting that you stick your head in the sand and hide from any of the fears that were mentioned in the opening paragraph. If you are concerned that the food you are eating might kill you; of course, you want to change that story. But, you also want to eat to please your belly-mind. Healthy food tastes good. Organic food is more enjoyable than non-organic. Natural foods are more gratifying than processed ones. Eat what truly feels wonderful to you, and release your food fears through the *five-step process*. If you find yourself in a situation of eating food that you know is not healthy for you, don't worry about it. It won't kill you, unless you want it to do so. Survival is not about purity. It is about loving yourself and your life so much that there is nowhere else you would rather be. Enjoy whatever you eat. If you love your food, your food will turn to love within you.

Many of you are worried about the effects of radiation, especially from mobile phones. If the fear is great, protect yourself until the *five-step process* has a chance to work. Then listen to your heart. If you are worried about your children's use of phones, I have a question for you. Which is the greater ultimate danger to your child, mobile phones or her brain-mind acting out of fear? Where are your priorities as a parent? You can hardly ask your children to surrender their fears to the belly-mind and to choose always to come from love unless you are making a sincere effort to do just that yourself. Kids aren't dumb. They'll smell that one a mile off.

When there is no fear and no denial, your love will create only from your heart's desire. There is nothing to fear. As you are building your love, take the precautions that you feel that you want. Ultimately there is no order of difficulties in miracles. When you are performing *Spiritual Alchemy*, there is no difference between creating a state of unconditional self-love (which you have experienced your ability to do, if you have worked with the process), and protecting yourself from nuclear war or a significant rising of the ocean levels. It doesn't matter where the fear of victimhood is coming from; love is simply the place where you begin. It helps, as you are dealing with what seem to be such enormous issues, to put things in perspective. If you believe that this body is all you get and then there is nothing, terror is more likely to hold you in its grip. If you hold the awareness that none of this is ultimately real, that it is just a big dream that you will awaken from someday, and that you will eventually laugh about it all – it is easier to let go of your brain-mind and find true peace and love in this very body. You are already ascended. Get used to it!

God Blesses You,

Sanhia

What are the real dynamics of rescuing?

Rescuing is a deeply ingrained part of your culture. You were raised with fairy tales about a damsel in distress, who is held captive by an evil knight or a dragon or a witch. The noble, good knight comes in to rescue her. What is communicated by this beautiful story? First of all, we have the hopelessness of the victim. The story does not recognize the victim as a powerful, infinitely creative child of God, but as a mere mortal of limited abilities – unable to help herself. Much can also be made out of the feminizing of the victim, but victims today can just as well be in a male as in a female body – though males may be less inclined to ask for help. Another aspect of the story is that there is some evil force outside of the victim that wishes to do harm to her, to exert power over her; and the victim is helpless in the face of this dark energy. If the rescuer is successful, which of course he usually is in these stories, what he has done is to confirm the powerlessness of the victim. The victim is forever indebted to the rescuer and the rescuer may look forward to a lifetime of protecting the victim. Regardless, the victim will continue to create situations where rescue is is seen as necessary. That is her story. The rescuer, also, will continue to look for damsels in distress.

The first question is to ask whether a great service is really being provided if the relief is only temporary. This is not to say that you are to ignore someone who is in danger or that support is not to be lent when the situation is grave. But if a pattern of helplessness exists, are you providing the highest service by continually rescuing? Jesus said that if you give a man a fish, you feed him for a day. If you teach a man how to fish, you feed him for a lifetime. When you rescue, you are giving a fish. Teaching victims how to rescue themselves feeds them for a lifetime. Jesus was able to heal others because he recognized their divinity. He did not see them as helpless victims. The key to eliminating victimhood lies in the recognition that you are the creative power in your life. As long as you pretend that you are not, you will always need rescuing. If you believe in victimhood, you will be one. If you think evil exists, it will continue to oppress you.

Without victims, there is no need for rescuers. Why would you rescue somebody if you recognized their divine power? Just what is the difference between the rescuer and the victim? They are two sides of the same story. One cannot exist without the other. It is the brain-mind that holds this story of helplessness. The only true rescue that can happen is for the brain-mind to choose to relinquish this story of victimhood. If it gives this powerlessness to the belly-mind to be embraced by its unconditional love, the illusion of fear can be transformed into spiritual gold. That rescue is not performed by another. It is accomplished by yourself. There can be aids or other support. When you create a new story, all kinds of assistance come to bring it into fruition, but those allies come at your order. They come because of your strength, not your weakness.

Rescuers can alleviate the pain, but a healing comes only from the wellspring of your own power and divinity. True rescuing involves supporting another's brain-mind to take its power. It does not provide solutions, but encourages others to create their own salvation. If the rescuer buys the story of the helplessness, the rescuer does not believe in the divinity of the victim. The rescuer sees the victim as weak and vulnerable. But, you cannot perceive powerlessness in another unless it is also part of your own story about yourself. Rescuing becomes a distraction. Instead of dealing with your own impotence, you deal with another's. There is a basic denial. But as you don't truly heal the victim's helplessness, you don't handle yours either. You pretend it is not there and project it upon another. This is the danger of being a rescuer. The world wants to pat you on the back, so there is a great sense of security in continuing to go out and rescue others. Your own feelings of weakness can be covered up. It feels safer to live in the illusion that you are strong and rescuing everyone else than to face your own fear. If the rescuer were to acknowledge the strength and divinity in the victims, what is left for them to do? How can you be a hero if there is nobody to save? The answer is that you can't truly rescue another until you liberate yourself. The task of the hero is to recognize his own divinity and to take full responsibility and power in his life.

Let us not forget the third leg of the victim triangle. We also need the villain, the victimizer. The play can't go on without one. Remembering that there can only be evil if you believe in it, what is the role of the villain? There needs to be a delivery system for the disaster that supports the belief in victimhood and helplessness. Without the victimizer, there is no painful "old story" to be freed from. The lack of belief in your personal divinity is still present, but there is no nagging need to release it. The villain is the answer to your prayers. You want to realize your divinity, but you need a situation that is so hopeless that you are ready to entertain the idea of changing your story. Part of the process of reclaiming your divinity is to welcome, thank, and give love to your victimizer. You have asked the villain to be there, whether you are aware of it or not. It could be no other way, because you are the divine power in your life. The victimizer is there to help you take your power. Thank you! Thank you! Thank you! In this story, it is important for the rescuer and the victim to give the villain his rightful place. The victimizer is showing them their mutual belief in evil. You have all taken your turns as the villain, whether consciously or not. You could not be in judgment of villains were you not also judging yourself. Whatever has been done to you, you have done to others. You are all in this story together, and all the parts are necessary. Embrace the victimizer within you with the unconditional love of your belly-mind.

Who is really stronger, the rescuer or the victim? The victim is confronting fears, while the rescuer may be denying them. Every human who has not recognized her divinity, her ascension, is a victim. That is the role she is playing. Those that recognize their victimhood have a chance for redemption. Those who believe in their role as a rescuer have little chance. Notice that in many of the rescuer stories there is a time of darkness for the hero. This is where the gold is hidden.

Notice when you attend spiritual groups that there are often more women present than men. The illusion of victimhood is more obvious for women in a patriarchal culture. Remember that being a victim is not your passport to ascension, but it often does lie between you and your awakening. Males who are successful in the material world have a particular challenge because they often have not experience themselves as victims. This is what Jesus meant when he said that it was easier for a camel to go through the eye of a needle than for a rich man to enter the kingdom of heaven. There is nothing random in the universe. There is purpose in everything. You are the creative power. Use the *five-step process* (see p. 230) or whatever works for you to let go of victimhood, take responsibility, and recognize your divinity. Be your own hero.

God Blesses You,

Sanhia

How can I realize my purpose?

This is the time of year when many of you take a vacation. The focus is on taking time for yourself, relaxing, and doing what you want to do. This often involves being out in nature. On one level, you are choosing to have a certain type of experience. It is like the sabbatical, which is an extended period for stepping out of your regular life, but it is more a place for playfulness and expression than for introspection. It is a time to enjoy life. Some of you experience less than pure joy on your vacations. A tremendous pressure can be felt to make the most of the time. For some there is the dread of the impending return to the "real world". This is particularly true for those of you who are not doing what you came here to do. It is as if the rest of your life is a sacrifice and the vacation has to fill all the empty holes in you. Then, at the end of the vacation you go back to a life that isn't chosen from your heart.

For those who are fully into your Right Livelihood, the Buddhist term used to describe following your heart in the work you do, there is a seamless flow from work into leisure. Vacation is simply another way of expressing your truth. But, for all it is a time of recharging, particularly in connection with the feminine energy. Let's look more closely at this term. Right Livelihood is connected to dharma rather than karma. It is not a balancing of energy from past and present life confusions, or karma; it is acting in harmony with your deeper being. There is something that you came here to do. It is yours and yours alone. Nobody else can do this, nor can you do anything else and know true peace. If you are not doing the thing you came here to do, there is a sense of failure and frustration about your life.

For some people, there is a total shut down around their purpose, but for many of you a piece of your purpose is visible to you, though not the whole. The challenge is to surrender fully to purpose. In the same way that you don't come in remembering your divinity, you also don't remember what you came to do. The remembrance comes through a conscious choice. If your commitment and habit is to choose love over fear, you will slowly uncover your Right Livelihood. When you are there, you are living in love. You are following your passion and sharing that love with others. What stands in the way is the belief that you don't deserve to do what you love to do. This may be expressed through a belief that the universe will not support you in following your heart. The ego voice in your head tells you, "You need to be serious. Buckle down. Keep your nose to the grindstone. You have to work hard to support yourself and your family. That's how it is." That is the voice, the belief, of fear and lack.

Part of following your Right Livelihood is to release the fear. But, an equal part is to truly know what your purpose is. These two are intertwined. If you carry a great deal of fear it may block the knowing. You may not be able to see it at all. You may think of yourself as someone with no particular gifts to offer the world. Or, you may see part of the picture but doubt your sanity and not trust what you see and feel. Those of you who live in western civilization are influenced by a mass consciousness that considers Right Livelihood to be a frill that can only be dallied with once you have taken care of the "meat and potatoes" of life, after you have done the duty that you owe to yourself, your family, and your society to work hard at something. But, the true service happens when you give from your divinity and share it with those who are close to you, your community, and the world. That is the greatest benefit you can offer, much grander than any self-sacrifice could provide.

How do you go about releasing fear and finding true purpose? A wonderful place to begin is with the *five-step process* (see p. 230). Your "old story" is whatever you believe to be true about Right Livelihood. It may be a statement of fear, one of confusion, or one of hopelessness. Feel where you are holding that energy in your body and focus your full attention upon it until you feel the unconditional love emerge. Then accept your divinity by taking full responsibility for your "old story", thanking it for its role in guiding you to your Right Livelihood. Finally, choose your new story from your heart. In addition to this process it will help to commit to bring something you love into your life each day. Set some time aside for yourself. Prime the pump with love until it begins to flow out of you constantly.

When we use the term "Right" this is not a judgment; it is a knowing. This is not to imply that there is a "Wrong" Livelihood. Right in this case means true to yourself. Only you know your purpose. Only you can feel it. It is like an inner GPS. No matter what direction you take in your life, this inner voice always points "right" to your purpose. It makes no difference how many painful steps may have been taken. Your inner compass will point you home. All there is for you to do is to wipe it clear of fear and let the love light your way. Let your vacation be a beginning. Choose to bring that special energy into every day of your life. You can do it on purpose.

God Blesses You,

Sanhia

Are aging and death certain?

Your birthday may not be soon, but you can apply this message to your most recent celebration or to your upcoming one. Take your pick. You are celebrating the illusion of being a year older. In the illusion, this day honors the day of your birth, of your beginning. The truth is that you are, you always have been, and you always will be. You simply are. The you that is has chosen to have the experience of being in a physical body without letting go of any part of your divinity. You are experiencing the "I Am" through the perspective of the physical. When you are not aware of your divinity, you have the illusion that life begins with your birth, cycles on through your lifetime, and ends with your death. After death, however, you will have a renewed awareness of your divinity, and will eventually plan another incarnation. From the human point of view this makes perfect sense, as you see all life around you going through these cycles. The whole universe seems to support this view of birth and death.

When you are not connected to your divinity you are very susceptible to the beliefs of the mass consciousness. The mass consciousness says, "A year older. Another ring on the tree. There are only so many rings. After a certain age, there will be a slow, but definite decline in the physicality. Finally, this will lead to your death, because the body is no longer a fun place to remain." This is the best scenario with the mass consciousness. It assumes a belief in life after death or a belief in future incarnations. However, if your life is ruled by fear, rather than love, the mass consciousness can take a worse turn. You may be alarmed by aging, frightened by the breaking down of the body, panicked at the inevitable death, and terrified that there is nothing beyond it. When you have the goal of ascension, the intention to fully realize your divinity, the limits to how you experience your physicality begin to drop away. As you experience your divinity, you find that time can move backwards as well as forwards. You can encounter life in multiple ways. You can travel to particular days in your life and re-experience them. Journey to other lifetimes is a possibility. There are no limits. I encourage you to take back the night. Let go of the darkness you hold around death and choose love.

When your birthday comes, make the choice to celebrate being a year younger. Decide to count backward each year until you reach your optimum age, whatever that might be. How do you want to experience the world? From what perspective of physical energy do you want to live? We can call this "youthing" or, to have fun with the English language, "youthanization". You begin by changing your stories about aging. The first one to change is the belief that your body will deteriorate. The new story could be that your body remains at a steady state, that you hold your present state of wellness. Like a bird in the wind, you can learn to fly in place. Learn that you can begin to reverse the aging process with your body.

In the mass consciousness, nothing is more certain than death. The slow (or sudden) deterioration of the body is a close second. There is no order of difficulties in miracles, but there is a greater challenge in creating a new story when the mass consciousness belief about the "old story" is strongly held. Are you willing to go against the beliefs of everyone you know? Unless you wish to run right into that wall, you might choose to work with youthing privately or only with those you trust at a deep spiritual level.

You cannot successfully choose youthing out of fear of death. When the motivation is fear, the realization cannot be divine. Remember that death is not real. You can never be destroyed. You are immortal. You choose life because you love life. You choose health because life is too much fun to play in any other way. You do this by accepting your divinity, by knowing there is only love, and by acting from that loving place. This is what the *five-step process* (see p. 230) is designed to support you in doing. It is not a ritual. A ritual is an action that you repeat, hoping that the gods will intercede on your behalf. That is not an acknowledgement of your divinity, but of your need for outside intervention. It is an act of hope, which is the flip side of hopelessness. The *five-step process* is an expression of your power, of your love (they are one and the same), and of certainty in your divinity. The motivation for youthing is not to live forever. It is to fully experience your divinity. Only when you are certain of your divinity can you know how long you wish to stay in your body.

As you are changing your story and taking full responsibility for your life, ask yourself what you want more than anything else. If the truth is that you wish to fully experience your divinity, to realize your ascension, everything else will take a back seat. All that comes into your life will be there to support you in fully knowing the truth of love. Here's to you, kid.

God Blesses You,

Sanhia

How important are special places and secret teachings?

There have always been special places on the planet which are known as power points, portals, energy vortexes, or by other names. You are still aware of many of them today. Some of you are drawn to Machu Picchu, Stonehenge, the Nile Valley with its pyramids and temples, Mount Shasta in California, the Himalayas and so on. Every continent has such places. People sought these locales out to make spiritual retreats, to fast, or to go on vision quests. These were times for purification and to get in touch with divine guidance. In some cases, spiritual communities evolved or developed near these power points, allowing the whole group to focus energy toward spiritual evolution.

At the same time, and often connected with these power places and/or their communities, there have been secret teachings. The spiritual knowledge was not written down. The secret teachings were not intended for the average person, who was not trusted to be able to safely handle such wisdom. It could prove to be self-destructive, or it might be used to gain power over others. If you wished to progress spiritually, you had to find a teacher. You had to prove your worth to that teacher. You couldn't simply enroll in a class, pay your fee, and be taught the secrets of the universe. You had to go through an initiation process, work at lower levels, and earn the trust of the teacher. They did not want to show you how to use spiritual power until you were ready for it. This is how it has been for eons. When the truths have been written down, they were done in such a way that the average person could not access them. Even when you read now the words assigned to Jesus in the Bible, some of which are accurate, they just hint at the fullness of his teachings. He only shared the deeper teachings with those who were ready to hear them. For others, they were hidden in parables or not dealt with in depth. Additionally, those who wrote down his words had only a partial understanding of them.

In 2012 the planet Earth completed its transition into ascension status. This is a change comparable to that initiated during the incarnation of Jesus and those who came to help in that work. A tremendous transformation has now taken place. Among the effects of this movement is that there is no longer a need for special places or for secrecy. You do not have to go to power points to access the divine energy. It is right here and it is right now. Wherever you are, it is. Your divine self is absolutely open to you. You don't have to go anywhere to find it. To seek it out in special places now can actually slow your process because it can reinforce the "old story" that you are separate from your divinity. I'm not suggesting that you never go to special places, only that there is no need to do so. If you feel a draw to a spot, then go. Follow your heart. There are no longer special places for the planet, but there may be special places for you. Only you can feel where those places are. You might realize, for example, that for your spiritual growth you desire a retreat in a place that provides peace and solitude. Perhaps you are led to live in such a place. Even then, there is not just one place that is the right one for you. Many can provide the solace you seek. Trust your heart and also what presents itself as you make your requests of Spirit.

The truth is now there for all to see and hear. The teachings are no longer hidden. You do not have to climb the mountain to find the guru to learn the secret of life. It is within you. You can turn on the television, walk into a bookstore, or look at the internet. The truth is everywhere. All the information is now out there in the open. Nothing is hidden. The only thing you have to do is to discern what is truth and what isn't. Listen with your heart. If the teaching is love based, it is likely true. If it is fear-based, it is likely false. If your intention is for experiencing your ascension, you will draw the truth to you.

There is no need for hiding the truth on this ascended earth. The shroud of secrecy has been lifted. Secrecy is based in fear. There is no longer a need to protect your truth from others. This is not to say that you are to proselytize the world. Live your own truth and share it with those who express interest. People who are holding onto fear energy can still create persecution and martyrdom. If you fear persecution, the tools are there to create safety about you. You can work with the *five-step process* (see p. 230) or other techniques. When you give up being a victim and claim your divine power, you are always protected.

People are still capable of twisting spiritual understanding to attempt to control others. The use of secrecy in the past to prevent this was unsuccessful. People still gained access to spiritual power and they took advantage of others. Yet earth survived because love is more powerful than fear. All that can be destroyed is that which is not real. Energy can only be used against those who agree to give their power away. It bears repeating. When you give up being a victim and claim your divine power, you are always protected.

You no longer need to seek out special teachers and to go through special initiations. If you draw to yourself a teacher who acts as if he holds the keys and presents that you have to show your worthiness to be his student, you may wish to take a step backward and breathe deeply. A true teacher makes you aware of your own divinity and your personal power. He encourages you to take responsibility. There are no wrong decisions, but some choices will bring more pain than others. The pain can always be a stimulus for growth, but is not a requirement for it. In the old energy, you needed to walk away from everyday life, from your family and community, in order to follow a spiritual path. Today, in the ascended energy you might choose to do that. You might choose to disappear for a while. But, none of this is absolutely necessary. The teachings are universally accessible. The divinity is within you wherever you might be. The choices are infinite and they are yours. Enjoy.

God Blesses You,

Sanhia

How can I step out of the mass consciousness?

We have talked a lot over the past messages about the *five-step process* (see p. 230), of your old stories and the changing of these stories. We have communicated that you are the power in your life; you are divine and create everything, whether consciously or unconsciously. Today let's focus on that part of the unconscious that we call the mass consciousness. These are the beliefs that permeate the culture in which you live. Most people simply accept these stories as true without questioning them, as if there *is* no choice. If you do question the mass consciousness, people might look at you as if you are crazy. You can travel to another culture and find differences in their mass consciousness. Some beliefs are nearly worldwide, the inevitability of death and taxes – for example. Health concerns are also part of the mass consciousness, such as the flu season or allergies. You might believe it is that time of year, so you are likely to catch something. Though many mass consciousness beliefs are universal, some ideas are narrower in scope, such as those running through families. There may be familial beliefs in good health as the standard, but other clans might hold illness and infirmities as often occurring events.

What we want to address today is the importance of being aware of the mass consciousness energy. Otherwise it will be running large parts of your life. Be particularly sensitive when you hear people, or perhaps even yourself, making statements that limit your spiritual power. Examples might include: "You just can't do what you want to do." "Nothing comes easy". "You have to fight to get what you want." "Money is evil." "You can't trust men /women." "Sex is bad/dirty/unholy/ going to get you in trouble." "I am getting old." "Don't rock the boat." I could go on and on. I won't. You already have available to you an overabundance of limiting mass consciousness beliefs. Notice these ideas as they come into your field of awareness, and instead of agreeing with them or promulgating them, ask yourself if this is a story you want to be true. If it isn't, you have your work cut out for you. Let go of that "old story" and choose a new one.

This is the place to use the *five-step process*. Your brain-mind is likely to cave in to some of these mass consciousness ideas and say "That is just the way things are." "People age." "Life is about suffering." It takes the second step where you confront the fear energy held in your body, before your brain-mind can successfully choose differently. It is not just a question of choosing a new story. It is a question of facing your fear of holding yourself up to the potential ridicule and anger of those around you. You will deal with the voices that say, "What makes you think that you can choose differently?" or "Who made you God?" Of course, the answer is that God made you God. You were made in the image of the infinite. You arc divine, *and*, you don't choose to have these old stories anymore. This is not to say that you are to share the new stories you are choosing with everyone. In fact, it is probably easier if you don't. It might be best to only disclose your new stories with those you trust to support you, until you find yourself strong in your divinity with confidence in your ability to choose your own stories. One of the great fears of stepping outside of the mass consciousness is that you will be crucified for it. That is an important story to change right away. Meanwhile, hold your cards close to your chest. Find a support group, even if it is but one person – "Where two or more are gathered in my name". Claim your divinity.

Walk away from the mass consciousness, whether it comes from religion, parents, governments, the media, science, or your own DNA. Change your story or it will run your existence because you are giving it permission to do so. Let's say a little bit more about the genetic coding of your DNA. There is the belief, greatly supported by the mass consciousness of science, that who you are is determined by what is in your genetic code; that your DNA is all-powerful. Your genetic code will be left behind in mother earth's compost pile while the truth of you goes on eternally. The immortal divine truth of you is always a greater power than your DNA. Your genetic code was created by the timeless truth of who you are. There was certainly purpose in that. You set things up in this life in order to have certain experiences, but you did not set yourself up to be a perpetual victim of those circumstances. If you have a situation that the mass consciousness says is genetically disposed – this is an opportunity, a spiritual gift, a place for you to say "I want to change that story".

You are all now having the opportunity to experience the changing of mass consciousness. Mass consciousness is not a static thing. It is not the same today as it was a thousand years ago, or even a hundred years ago. When a critical mass of people hold a new story, the mass consciousness begins to change. It requires only a small minority of people holding the new story to effect this transformation. It was such a critical mass that brought the earth into an ascended state, and that ascended state now allows the mass consciousness to change more quickly (see Message 25 *What about the planetary ascension of 2012?*). It is easier now for people to choose a new story than it was fifty years ago. There is less resistance. Not only are you altering your stories more easily, but you are replacing more stories and more people are choosing to convert their stories. This has a snowball effect. Changes in mass consciousness that used to take a century can now occur in five years. The current change in technology is mirroring the change in mass consciousness.

Perhaps the greatest block remaining for you in the mass consciousness is the fear of your divinity. You believe that to fully claim your divinity, and, therefore your power, is blasphemy. There is a belief that such a desire is evil or satanic, that it is of the ego or a sign of mental illness. To claim your divinity, to realize you are the power in your life and can do whatever you wish to do, is a heresy. That is the greatest fear. People are terrified of taking their power, or of even asserting they have a divine right to claim it. This is the mass consciousness promulgated by most religions. It was not the teaching of Jesus. He spoke of his achievements by saying "this and more you shall do". The truth is out there in many published books. There are people talking and writing in the mass media. There are workshops and classes. This energy was almost invisible fifty years ago, but it is everywhere today. The energy supporting the recognition of your personal divinity is there. The critical mass is close. It is becoming easier, but nobody can make the choice for you. Ultimately, you, yourself, will come face to face with your fear and find the love behind it. I'm on your side. I've got your back. But, you have to be brave enough to claim your freedom. Choose to unlock the shackles of mass consciousness.

God Blesses You,

Sanhia

Why is intention necessary?

Many of you celebrate the birth of Jesus. There is a great deal of confusion about who Jesus was and what his significance is for us today. What Jesus came to show us and to demonstrate is our personal divinity, that we are children of God as he is. That is the message. It is one of resurrection, not of self-sacrifice and martyrdom. However, you hold this belief in suffering in your bodies. The crucifixion story was written down and passed on in its present form because that was the energy that mankind was holding 2000 years ago. Martyrdom could be accepted, but the divinity of people was not part of anybody's story. It threatened all existing orders.

The picture of God that is held by many people today still has nothing to do with the essence of unconditional love and unlimited potential that is the divine creative force. We were made in the image of this God. What has happened, in the popularly accepted view, is that God has been created in the image of man – man in ignorance of the truth of his divinity. All the negative emotional energies that are held in a fear-based life are projected upon God – an angry, punishing, judging, jealous God.

We want to recall that there is one overriding message that Jesus came to teach, that we are divine. We are the power in our lives. We create everything that happens. How do we do this? Some of the truth was recorded. He said to ask and it will be given. You must ask. It comes from intention. This is what we want to talk about today. You created a planet of free will where you can choose anything that you want. You cannot unchoose the truth of your divinity, because that exists above and beyond this physical earth, without limit. Nothing can destroy you or another human soul. You have choice only over your experience here. Once you leave, the veil lifts and the emotional baggage you were carrying is gone. Here you have a choice. You can opt for fear or love. If your intention is to go with fear, your experience will justify your selection. Everything that happens to you will prove the correctness of your intention.

If you do not intend to claim your divinity, you will continue to deal with pain and suffering. Experiencing your divinity is not likely to happen accidentally. You begin with the intention. You must ask. But, simply asking without taking action can make for a very slow realization of your divinity, one that might not be fulfilled in your present incarnation. You have all of this fear energy in your body. You are carrying it with you from this and former lifetimes. It continues to manifest negative emotional experiences where you have depression, anger, hopelessness, jealousy, or fear of lack. It helps to have your aim be true and consistent.

It is not enough for your brain-mind to think that you are divine. There are many wonderful books out there about the spiritual nature. Reading them will not give you an experience of your oneness with God, nor will reading this message. Your timelessness is experienced as you transform the emotional energy that is held in your body, and your brain-mind is incapable of doing that. You cannot think your way out of this. Affirmations will not bring about the realization of your holy nature. You carry this energy in your body, not in your mind. Your brain-mind reacts to the emotional energy in your body in a slavish manner. It is an endless loop. You create situations out of the beliefs you hold. Then you have a negative emotional reaction to the situation, and your brain-mind jumps right in. It chooses blame and victim thinking. Your brain-mind may try to squelch the negative emotion in the body, but it fights a losing battle. In the end, it is not about changing your mind or thoughts. Intention is about taking action in alignment with Spirit.

You certainly want to act out of love and your true desire. In order to do this, let go of self judgment and move to unconditional acceptance. No matter what. The fear you are holding in your body refuses to allow you to do that. The ego is basically screaming out, "Without me you are nothing. I am all that is protecting you from oblivion!" It is an impossible task to successfully argue with this fear that doesn't believe in your divinity. You can only embrace it with love. What is required is an intention to not try to cover up, hide from, or change this energy of fear in your body. Have the intention to love it, to welcome it, and to simply watch it. If you observe it for long enough with acceptance, the fear transforms to love. It is that simple, because it always was love. That is all that is real. The fear is an illusion. We have just described the <u>second step</u> of the *five-step process* (see p. 230). This is what we call *Spiritual Alchemy*, the transforming of fear into love.

The commitment is to do the process with the fear-based emotions every time they come up – until they stop surfacing, until all that is left in your reaction to every situation is love. You will continue to create the situations that will trigger your fear until it is dissipated. Then those same situations, if they were to arise, would be answered only with love. At that point when your response to everything is love, the question may arise – "has the world changed or is it my reaction that has altered?" The truth is that both have transformed. There is no difference. There is no separation.

If you feel that you are responding only with love, but you buy into others' illusions – you see them as hopeless, sad, or victims – you are projecting your own fears. That energy is still present; the other person is simply holding up a mirror for you. Take the feelings they trigger for you. Silently thank the other for showing you what you are still holding and go back to work on yourself. You cannot change the experience for anybody else. This is the planet of free choice. Everyone has the right to be a victim and to suffer – as you have the birthright to be fully free and claim your divinity. It is not your job to do this for anybody but you; but it is your job to see them as divine, no matter how they perceive themselves.

Christmas is a wonderful time to celebrate the birth of your awareness of your divinity. In the dark of the year you can shine your spiritual light on your own darkness. Allow it to be there and embrace it with your love. Every candle you light can be a symbolic gesture toward this commitment to loving your emotions. You are divine.

God Blesses You,

Sanhia

Do I have to choose between spirituality and sexuality?

There are many people who would never put spirituality and sexuality in the same sentence unless they were talking of contrasts or differences, but certainly not when speaking about any commonality of energy. We wish to speak today about the spirituality of sexuality. Before we begin, it would be helpful if you would go back and read Message 33 *Is it helpful to honor the feminine energy?*

What we call spiritual energy deals with the communication between the physical world and the divine. We could say that spirituality is an attempt by people to connect with their divine side. From the perspective of your eternal or higher self, which does not deal with the physical realm, there would be no focus on spirituality. It would be like fish talking about water. That is the "isness" of eternal existence. The divine nature is simply what is. Spirituality as a specific topic is only of interest to those aspects in a physical body. It is only for those who have forgotten their eternal natures. One belief that has evolved over time is that the only way to realize your divinity is to deny your physicality. Many religions have picked up on this and have chosen to forbid certain physical actions. They might say that you can't eat certain foods, that you shouldn't enjoy yourself too much, or that you shouldn't seek after physical pleasure. The ultimate admonitions are strictures against human sexuality.

The belief of those who wish to deny the fleshly pleasures is that the physical is evil and only the spiritual is good. From that point of view there can just be pain and suffering in the physical. The only salvation is in death. This leads to a great confusion. Why even be born? Why come into this evil physical existence? Who has created this wickedness? If it is God who has created the physical, what possible reason could God have for creating evil? It's perplexing. From this perspective, the greatest evil of all is sexuality. Without sexuality, no more beings are introduced into this hell. This ultimate spiritual direction was expressed by the Shakers who eliminated sex entirely. Though other religions have not gone that far, most have judgments and restrictions around sexual energy. The more fundamentalist a religion is, that is, the more they believe in a masculine and/or judging God, the more censure and condemnation there is about sexuality. Because it is the women who bring the new beings into the physical world, there is more judgment directed at them.

Let us look at what this sexuality is really about. When we let go of judgment – of thoughts of right and wrong or good and evil – and we accept the perfection and purpose in everything, what is the function of sexuality? The sensual experience has a great potential to open you up to your own divinity. Erotic encounters allow you to absolutely let go of everything that is not present and sense the energy within the physical form of your body. It allows you to feel unconditional love and ecstasy. Sexuality can help you on the way to realizing your ascension, but no amount of sex will guarantee the knowingness of your divinity or your ascension. Of course, also, no amount of judging or harnessing your sexual nature will lead you to the knowing of your true self, either.

What we encourage first of all is that you let go of whatever judgments you may have about your sexuality. Become aware of issues of control, whether it is your domination of others or your fear of being manipulated. Notice the places where you feel yourself to be a victim of sexuality. Feel that energy in your body and use the *five-step process* (see p. 230) to transform it into love. Choose the story you wish to have about your sexual nature in the fourth step. Embrace your sexuality as a full part of your divinity. One of the reasons that you chose to create this physical universe and to come into your body was to deal with sexuality.

Some of you have had incarnations where the main purpose was to experience as much sexual energy as you could. In other lifetimes, you have experimented with having no sexual activity to see what that was like. There is no goodness or badness about this. You are free to choose whatever you want. I am not telling you how much sex you are to have. It is your spiritual heart that will tell you that. It is to that place where you are coming from love rather than fear that you wish to listen. You will know that you are honoring the truth for you when you realize that you are free of any judgment for how others conduct their sexual lives. There is no one way to be around sex. The "one truth" idea leads to the belief in right and wrong. The one truth is that you are divine, infinitely loving, and creative, and that you are absolutely unique as an immortal divine being. You are to express your divinity and your uniqueness through a physical vehicle by having physical events. To deny your sexuality is to deny your spirituality.

As you give yourself permission to fully explore your sexuality, you may tap into vast reservoirs of fear that have been lodged in your body. That is a wonderful thing to discover. You have been carrying that energy in your body for lifetimes. There is nothing more intertwined with judgment on this planet than sexuality. Therefore, there is nothing with greater potential to set you free than is your healing around sexuality. Confront those fears. Find your divinity. Whatever stories you have in your mind that great spiritual leaders were non-sexual is an illusion. These stories are passed down by those with their own sexual issues. Sexuality was a part of the spiritual process for Jesus, Buddha, and nearly every other ascended being. Please enjoy the rest of your trip.

God Blesses You,

Sanhia

How do violence and guilt relate to sexuality?

In the last message we spoke of spirituality and sexuality. There are two issues dealing with this subject that we would like to go into today. The first has to do with the coincidence of sexuality and violence. The second concerns undesired pregnancies. There is a connection between the two issues, but we will begin by looking at them separately. Deep within many of you there is a belief that sexual energy is not divine. To partake in sexuality is therefore to separate yourself from God, and, therefore, comes punishment somewhere down the line.

Violence is not an expression of sexuality. Sexuality is an energy that comes from the sharing of love. We wish to disconnect violence and sex in your brain-mind. Rape is violence; it is not sexual. It comes out of fear, not love. Love never requires another to do something that isn't freely chosen. Fear can draw one to violate the freedom of another, or at least to attempt to, whether that violation is verbal, physical, or spiritual. Verbal and physical abuse are well understood. Spiritual abuse includes curses and spells, as well as the use of spiritual powers to encourage another to behave in a sexual way with you. As we have mentioned before, the development of spiritual powers is not always connected with love and spiritual maturity.

Let us again draw a line in the sand and say that when we are talking about rape or sexual violence we are not talking about sexuality. However, for many of you, particularly those who have chosen to incarnate in a feminine body, there is an emotional difficulty in separating these two – particularly if you have created the experience of apparent victimhood to sexual assault. Then you might find it difficult to have a sexual experience based in love, because the fear energy is still strongly held in your body. We want to remind you that when we talk about creating situations, it is never a statement of blame. If you are holding guilt or blame for the situation that happened, it is not our intention to support that. We wish to remind you of the absolute truth that you are the divine power in your life and that nothing could possibly happen without your permission. This does not mean that your intention or permission was consciously granted to the sexual violence that you have experienced or that you have fear of. You may wish to use the *five-step process* (see p. 230) to feel this fear of sexual violence in your body, go into it and embrace this terror until it transforms to love; then visualize a new reality for yourself. This allows you to let go of victimhood and take your true power.

For some of you, your identification with victimhood is so much a part of who you believe yourself to be that you are unaware of having it. Here are some signs to look for. Do you feel something holding you back from sexual activity, aside from lack of interest in a particular possible partner? Do you find yourself having strong emotional reactions when watching films or television shows (or in reading novels or following true life stories) portraying sexual violence? Do you find yourself getting angry at the perpetrator or in judgment of the victim? "How could they let that happen?" " How could they be so stupid?" If you do, your belief in your victimhood is active. If you have not created an ongoing fulfilling sexual relationship in your life, the fear energy is probably present, and likely not just from this incarnation but from many lifetimes. This is a major reason why lasting, loving relationships are not created. For others, the guilt creates a chain of violent partners.

Now let's look at the male side of the equation. Here it is more likely that you have guilt about sexuality because you believe it is wrong. That begs the question for you, "What woman would want to do that?" So, you either deny yourself sex or feel you have to trick or force the woman into the sexual experience. Tricking might mean making promises that you don't intend to honor. Force, of course, means rape – which could mean emotional or mental force, as well as physical. All of this emerges out of the belief that you don't deserve to have physical intimacy, so the only way to have it is through force. "What woman would want to have sex with you?" None, so you need to use some form of coercion." And what kind of woman is going to have sex with you?" Only an evil woman, separated from God and spirituality would do that nasty thing with you. Now your use of force is somewhat justified. But what are your prospects for a lasting, supportive, loving committed relationship? "How can you commit to a relationship with a woman that you don't respect?" If you do make love, you will be punished. Perhaps, she will control you and ruin your life in return for sex. Or, you can use the *five-step process*. For the woman, there may be the belief that there must be a relationship in order to have financial security. Sex can be seen as a price that has to be paid in order to have that support. Quite a story isn't it! The good news is that you are both free. You don't have to act out this story anymore. You can just let it go.

Before we leave for today, let's talk about the subject of unwanted pregnancy, which affects both of you – although the woman has a larger role. For the man, the fear is likely to be that the pregnancy is going to rope you into the relationship and you may have to make a commitment. Even if there is already a child or two, the noose is being tightened and the responsibilities and restrictions are increasing. Unwanted pregnancy is the consequence you knew was coming from having sex. The extreme in the mass consciousness tells you that the only excuse for sex is reproduction and that you must live with your sinful choices and have the baby. Even if those religious structures don't exist for you, it is likely that you believe that you have no control over pregnancy, short of abstinence. Most forms of artificial birth control carry with them some danger from side effects. Guilt is there with or without religion. The purest form of birth control is to love yourself unconditionally and to process all of your sexual guilt through the *five-step process*. Choose conception consciously. This is a big step. In the meantime, take prudent precautions until you are clear that you have released the fear and judgment from your body. Affirmations alone will not do that. Don't come back to me and say, "Sanhia, you told me I wouldn't get pregnant unless I wanted to". If you do create an undesired pregnancy, there is no right or wrong choice. You will learn and grow from either. The potential child is an immortal soul (and old buddy) who has agreed to play this role for you. Either way, that soul will continue.

The *five-step process* is a very powerful and effective tool. But, that does not mean that it is necessarily easy for an individual to succeed at it the first time she tries. Some of you have more innate skill in doing the process by yourself. For many, it may be helpful for somebody to guide you, somebody in whom you have confidence. You may also use the recording at www. channelswithoutborders.com/5-step-process/. It all comes down to you and to your intention. The tools are there to use. If you prefer the support of another, create that. Find a partner and support each other. There is always a way. It is the strength of your intention that makes the difference. We love you. We wish you to have a wonderful experience in physicality and to free yourself from all the fears of sexuality so that you may enjoy it ecstatically.

God Blesses You,

Sanhia

What do you mean when you say I pre-planned this life?

Let's start today by talking about the truth of who you are. You are divine. You are one with God. You are the creator of all that is in the physical realm. This cannot be stated too many times. When you crossed the threshold and moved into the physical vessel of this body that you have created for your earthly experience, you forgot who you are. You think that you are less than divine and go on to prove yourself right. Just because you don't believe in or can't accept your godliness, you don't stop being divine. You simply create from this stepped down point of view. You generate the illusion of limits throughout your life.

Let's take a step back across the threshold, to a point before you created this incarnation. You now have a greater awareness of your divinity. Having been through this cycle of birth and death many times, and knowing how forgetful you become when you get back into a body, you try to design things to wake you up. You want to make yourself aware of the truth of who you are while you are in this next body. You hope to ascend. We call this pre-planning. This is where you, along with those souls who have decided to incarnate with you and play significant roles in your life, make agreements.

It is helpful for you to take to heart and understand that the pre-planned future events may look like disasters to you. Things may happen in your life that you would never consciously choose, such as accidents, death, loss of a love, or material setbacks. When you look at these events from the point of view which has forgotten your divinity, you might think that you are a victim of a random – or worse – cruel world. Why is this happening to me? Is God punishing me? The answer is that you planned it this way, that you are the god you have been railing against. You hoped these events would shake up your life so you could perceive yourself differently and begin to recognize your divine nature.

If everything in your life worked out well, you would be fairly content most of the time. You would be okay. If your parents were good enough, if you were relatively smart and healthy, if you had decent physical coordination and were attractive to others, if people liked you and you had plenty of friends, and if you were satisfied with your partner – you would be okay. If you had healthy, intelligent children who didn't give you too much hell, a talent and job that you mostly enjoyed and which brought you a comfortable income, life would be okay; but spiritually, you might not grow at all. Why rock the boat? There is nothing wrong with such a life unless it is your desire to experience your true essence, not just "good enough". If you want to experience divinity and the absolute truth of who you are, and use your infinite individualized creativity to affect this earth plane and others in it, "good enough" is not good enough. That is not what you came to do. You pre-planned events and relationships to guide you in the ascension direction you wanted to follow, knowing that you would forget this course once you got into a body.

Look at your life now and find the one, or perhaps two or three, traumatic events that cause you to say to yourself that in no way did you choose this. Take responsibility for those events as you do in the third step of the *five-step process* (see p. 230). State that you chose this story, not to punish yourself, but out of love. This is recognition of your intention. While it is important to choose your new stories and to create the life you desire, it is equally important to realize that every story you already have comes from an intention. If you deny that intention, you deny a whole side of your divinity. Take these "worst" events to your heart one at a time and do the *five-step process* with them. Feel where the story is held in your body and fully experience the energy until the *Spiritual Alchemy* does its work. Sometimes with these big stories, the energy is so powerful it feels like it doesn't want to let go. This is a place where it can help to dialogue with the energy. Welcome it into your body. Thank it for being there. Acknowledge that you asked it to come. Tell it that you know it has a gift or a message for you and express your willingness to receive and to act on that guidance.

If your intention is to realize your ascension and get there in the most direct manner possible, embracing these events that seem the most challenging is the quickest way to go. Look the event in the face; tell it, "I chose you. Thank you for being here. If it weren't for you I wouldn't be here asking to recognize my divinity." When you can transform your greatest failure into your greatest success, anything is possible. And it is.

God Blesses You,

Sanhia

What can help me to forgive?

I have referred to mirrors off and on through the years. Those of you who have worked with me directly have heard me talk about them. Now it is time to give the subject some deep reflection (pause for laughter). Jesus spoke of mirrors. He said to remove the log in your own eye before judging another. He also said, "judge not, lest ye be judged". He had much more to say on the subject, but the writers of the New Testament didn't know what to do with the information – they didn't understand it – so it didn't make the final cut.

We can begin by saying that everything that is physical is not real. Your ego is telling you that what you see and touch is real, but it is not. That which is real exists forever. Everything that is physical is temporary. Where does the physical come from? It comes from you. You have created it. When I say you, I am talking to you, the individual reading these words. Everything, without limit, that exists in the material realm is your creation. God has nothing directly to do with it. God created you. You created the earth. This is your game. Again, I am talking to you specifically, not people in general. You have the illusion that everybody is experiencing the same physical "reality", but if you check out any of your stories with anybody else who was "there", the tales don't completely line up. If your political affiliation differs, they may not line up at all. No two people ever experience the same thing. You each have your own illusions. There are places where there is a great agreement in your stories; we call this mass consciousness. But there are also areas of great disagreement about the illusion. However, the ego believes that it is all reality rather than illusion.

The ego asks what the purpose of all this is if it is not real. It doesn't want to hear an answer, and there is no answer that would satisfy, because the answer is, "None". If your ego were to fully accept the meaninglessness of your physical experience it would have to accept that it, also, has no purpose and it would disappear. All the ego does is to keep you believing in your separation from God and from your divinity. The ego cannot exist in the space of unconditional love. When you are in a permanent state of unconditional love, all you do is channel your divinity. Your ego stays out of the way. It disappears. You continue to operate in the physical realm, but you don't take it seriously. You recognize that it is not real. What can possibly upset you if nothing is real? Instead the world becomes a place where your divinity plays. Your divinity created this illusion as a tool for your ascension, not for you to be fooled into taking it seriously. When you absolutely realize that it is not real, that everything physical is an illusion – you will have realized your ascension.

But we came here to talk about mirrors. If you wish to go the shortest distance or take the least time to experience your divinity and release your ego, it is quite productive to work with the concept of mirrors. It goes like this. Everything that exists in your physical world, including yourself, is your creation. Your ego thinks everything and everyone else is separate from you. They are not. Their physicality is your creation, as yours is theirs – but that is none of your business. When you observe another's actions, what you see is you, not them. That's all you can see. Everything you see around you is you. You are the creator. If you find yourself in judgment of someone's actions, it is yourself you are judging. I can hear your ego at work already saying, "What do you mean! I would never kill someone, or start a war, or kick someone when they are down. I would never do that." Yes, you would. In fact, you have already done it – though perhaps it was in a previous life – and you haven't forgiven yourself. You are still judging yourself. In fact, you can't even look to see it within yourself because you have so much judgment. So, you produce a "scapegoat". You create somebody else to commit the action you can't forgive in yourself. The game the ego plays is to judge others instead of judging yourself. When you understand that, you know there is not even a reason to forgive, let alone to judge anyone else. They are simply doing as you have bid them. In fact, what you can do is to bow down to that person and thank them for showing you what you were unable to see in yourself. Thank you! Thank you! Thank you! Now you can forgive it in yourself. Whatever you did had no permanent effect. Nothing real was hurt because nothing real can be hurt. There is nothing to forgive.

Once you have taken ownership of the action you have judged in another, do whatever you can to forgive yourself, starting with having the intention to do so. The *five-step process* (see p. 230) is always helpful here. When you realize that nobody has ever done a thing to you, that it has always been your creation and that, beyond that, none of it matters – you are realizing the truth of who you are. None of it matters. All that matters is love. It is that simple. This is what the mirror is about. It doesn't matter if you see something, hear about it, or read about it. It doesn't matter if it is "truth" or fiction, whether you see it on TV or in a movie, or read about it in a novel. It makes no difference. Wherever you find your mirror, your job is to let go of the outwardly directed judgment and to acknowledge that this is where you judge yourself. This is where you have the illusion of guilt and separation from God, even though God never experiences any separation or judgment. Never. It's not in the job description. God is unconditional love and unlimited creativity. That's it.

Out of your unlimited creativity you have manifested this physical illusion and placed yourself in it in such a way that you have forgotten who you are. It's a maze and you have been trying to find your way out of it. The way out is to realize there is no maze. Use your mirrors to get out. See where your illusions lie. Forgive yourself. Find love and laugh a lot. The illusion is pretty funny when you stop thinking about it.

God Blesses You,

Sanhia

Why is it important to balance my masculine and feminine energy?

All of you in Western Civilization pay homage to the masculine above the feminine. This is not a criticism; it is simply an "isness". There is nothing wrong with paying homage to the masculine, but when this devotion is out of balance with your homage to the feminine it is difficult to realize your ascension, to realize your own divinity, because you are denying half of yourself. I want to talk a bit about the masculine and the feminine so that you can be sensitive to when they are operating in your life and where your emphasis is, so that you can choose to move that focus if you wish.

The irony of my job – I do have a job that I love to do – is that I do a bit of a bait and switch act. I come in the form of one who seems to be of masculine energy, not only coming through a male channel but also having ascended in a male body, to people on a conscious spiritual path who honor the masculine. Though gender is not the truth of who I am, I play the male role very well. People listen because they respect that air of masculine divinity, even if they are angry about it and hate men. They still respect it on an unconscious level. Everyone does. My job is to use my masculine authority to convince you to listen to your feminine side. That is the irony. And it's a lot of fun, because nothing matters more than your feelings. And that is the connection to your feminine side – what you are feeling. It doesn't matter whether you are happy, stressed, or angry. Your feelings are important. If you don't love and accept those feelings in yourself, you are denying the feminine.

The masculine spiritual energy doesn't say, "Don't listen to that bitch". There is no battle between them. The energy of the masculine pole is to show light. "This is who you are. This is what you can do. Your mind is creative." Of course, all of this is true. But what is missing is that if you don't love yourself, your mind is absolutely helpless to accomplish what you want in your life. The power of creation requires the feminine and the masculine to work together, the light of the masculine and the unconditional love of the feminine. None of you have any problem with the "light" part. You have all followed teachers and read books. You have become inspired and want to follow some direction, and then you fail. You are not able to do it. You decide that you are inferior to the teacher or the author. It seemed so easy when you were in the class and were told that all you had to do was this..... It is not about the "brain-mind" knowing.

It is about feeling the love. This is why we created the *five-step process* (see p. 230). Notice that the process doesn't start out with your new story. It doesn't start from the light. It starts from the "old story", from the pain, the fear, and the separation. In the second step, your job is to go into those feelings, into the feminine aspect, and to love them. If you go into the pain and you tell yourself that you are doing it because you want to get rid of it, you are throwing the baby out with the bath water. Whatever the feeling is, if your desire is to simply avoid it, you are not honoring the feminine. Rather than running away from or pushing away the feelings in the second step, you go directly into them. You face the energy and fully experience it; you merge with, welcome, listen to, love, and thank it for being there. You ride and stay with it wherever it goes through your body, however strong it gets, and in whatever way it might morph. The feeling always has a message or a gift for you. You may not always speak with the energy on a verbal level to get that message. The communication might be subtle, symbolic, or a vision. If your brain-mind is still engaged at this point of the process, it can be most helpful to have a dialogue with the energy in your body so that you can let go of judging, analyzing, and labeling the feeling – allowing you to receive that message. Eventually the feeling will transmute to the unconditional love of the feminine belly-mind. You feel this inner warmth, not because you ran from your feelings, but because you dove into them. When you choose your new story in the fourth step, you are not choosing it from your "brain-mind". You are choosing it from your heart, from the merging of the feminine and the masculine. You just know that this is your new story.

The feminine comes first, not second. You cannot be here in a physical body without coming through your mother. This doesn't mean that the feminine is more important; they are both absolutely necessary. Love simply comes first. This flies in the face of the mass consciousness of Western Civilization which states that masculine energy always leads. It doesn't. It follows. This does not mean that women are always to lead. You all have both feminine and masculine energy within you. The primary job of the masculine is to empower the feminine.

The masculine is to lead in such a way as to make it safe to experience your feelings. For the most part, the masculine has been doing just the opposite. It has taken its task to be the chasing away of feelings. "Don't cry. I will make everything alright. Don't look at your fears. Just look at the light. Think positively!" For the masculine to truly lead would be to encourage the crying of all the tears and the expression of all the fears. We are not referring to the projection of the fears upon others or a blaming. We speak of an encouragement to fully feel them without defending, rationalizing, or judging. Use your masculinity to support the full experience of your femininity. When you find the unconditional love that lies beneath everything else in you, your masculine can truly choose what you want. You don't want to avoid pain; you want to fully experience love. They are not the same thing. When the masculine is separate from the feminine, it thinks it has to stay in charge and make the choices. Otherwise all hell might break loose. But, when your masculine is in touch with the unconditional love of your feminine, it gives up control and says to Spirit, "What do you want me to do?" And that guidance always leads to exactly what you really want. It's beautiful. You are not doing it out of a sense of self-protection, but out of a recognition of purpose. It's an absolute surrender and yet an assertion of your masculine energy. It's doing what you came here to do. Your "brain-mind" will never discover that by itself. Such awareness comes when you fully accept all your feelings and everything Spirit sends to you. You let the transformation take place where you feel the unconditional love of the feminine. Then you can see the light.

God Blesses You,

Sanhia

Is there divinity in everyone?

I would like to suggest a small procedure for each of you to practice in addition to the *five-step process* (see p. 230). As you go through your day and different people come into your awareness, attempt to see their divinity. Some people may present a larger challenge for you than others. You may find yourself having a judgment about a person for some reason. Remember to be aware that he or she is your mirror, and it is with yourself that you have the judgment. Then you can use the *five-step process* to work with that energy. But, you can also try to stay present and see that person as divine. Remind yourself that no matter what they are doing, what they have created, or what energy they are putting out – all is perfection. The truth of them is divine and whatever is happening has the purpose of helping you to realize that.

There is a habit of unconsciousness. Unconsciousness means not being aware of your divinity. It becomes a routine to go through your day and not think about your divinity. It can be a pattern, beyond that, to obsess with things that are diametrically opposed to the idea of divinity – things such as sadness, lack, unhappiness, fear, and so on. Seeing the divinity in others is simply a discipline to help you become conscious instead of unconscious. As you are going through your day and you become aware of someone, let's say a stranger, you may react in a habitually protective manner. You are careful not to show yourself until you find out who this person is. You might feel threatened by them. Often you are looking at this being from a place of judgment. Do you like this individual or not? Is this somebody you can connect with? Is this human enlightened? What we are suggesting is a whole new way of observing a stranger. Instead of looking at them with eyes of judgment and fear, look at them with the eyes of unconditional love. Instead of looking at them from the brain-mind, look at them from the belly-mind. This doesn't mean that you try to ignore or repress any uncomfortable feelings you get around this person. If you have such a reaction, you keep looking at this soul from your belly-mind and love them unconditionally. You accept them fully as they are. Your brain-mind has only one job now, and that is to say that this person is divine as you are divine. This being is a piece of God. This individual is an eternal immortal soul. Perhaps the person is unconscious of their divinity. Remind yourself of the truth, so that you can look upon this soul with the eyes of unconditional love and acceptance, seeing or at least looking for their divinity.

If what you are experiencing with this soul does not feel divine, your process is to let go of your brain-mind, because it doesn't seem to be helping right now. Coming from your belly mind, send them unconditional love. Silently express this acceptance and seek the understanding that they are in your life to deliver an important message to you. Let go of the fear you have of their message and welcome it. Your process is to accept the other. This is like a walking meditation. See the perfection in everything and everyone you meet.

The process can be even more challenging when practiced with your friends and loved ones. Here you have a history of a pattern of judgments and ways of reacting. You already have a big story in which they play an assigned role. It can be harder to let go of your unconsciousness with those close to you than with your perceptions of a stranger. In fact, your judgments of strangers often are directly related to the way in which they remind you of somebody you know. Keep looking at your friend. See who they are and love that person unconditionally. Imagine what a joy it would be to realize that you are traveling around with divine friends, that your partner is divine and that your family members and coworkers are divine. What a difference that would make! What a supportive world you would have to live and play in.

This process of seeing the divinity of others is not limited to when they are in your physical presence. There are also the times when others come into your thinking or your brain-mind. Be conscious at these times, also. Are you being judgmental in your thoughts? Are you upset with them? Are you worried about them? Remind yourself of their divinity. This is a piece of God that has taken human form, just like you have. In the face of this divinity, how do you now look at their actions? The first thing, of course, is to affirm their divinity. Secondly, take responsibility for any difficulty you are experiencing, knowing that has to do with you and not with them. Finally, ask for support from your guides, angels, higher self, inner knowingness, and from Spirit to help you understand how and why this is divine. Find a way of seeing the perfection of what is transpiring.

Practice seeing that perfection and divinity in everyone you meet each day, friend or stranger. Where do you see the divinity in this individual? What do you appreciate about this being? In the discipline of doing that you will begin to see yourself in a conscious way. All of the time. When you see the perfection of what is happening, you stop taking others' drama seriously. You won't get drawn into their story of victimhood or lack of divinity. You may pay attention to it, but you know what it truly is. You may or may not share this awareness, based on how receptive the person is to hearing it, but your reaction no longer fuels their old story. Otherwise, there is nothing for you to do but to recognize the perfection and the divinity.

One of the beauties of looking for the divinity in others is that you can't change their actions. With yourself, you have the illusion that there is something you should change. You believe that if you could just be different, you might experience your divinity. With others, you have no power to change them. All you can do is to love them as they are. What a gift that is. Seeing the divinity of others is a perfect complement to the *five-step process*, which is a way to accept yourself unconditionally. If you remember to practice acceptance with just one soul today, and perhaps with another tomorrow and each day thereafter, you will experience a profound movement. Why don't you start with the next person you see or happen to think of? You are simply divine!

God Blesses You,

Sanhia

What can I do when things are less than perfect?

In the last message I talked about seeing divinity in every person. This time I want to look at seeing perfection in everything. We will begin with a definition of perfection, starting with what it is not. Perfection is not the result of endless tweaking. Constantly adjusting, changing, and working with things does not create perfection. This is the product of the ego's judgment. I would reverse that thinking. You simply acknowledge that how it is now, is perfection. How it is, how it was, and how it will be – all of these are perfection. Since everything is perfect as it is, everything is divine.

If perfection is a standard that has to be reached, divinity would be hard to realize. Rather than trying to change the outside, change your perception. Take a different view of your past. Each of you had perfect parents. They could not have been better. You could not have chosen better parents – and you did choose them. You chose perfect friends as you were growing up; you chose perfect teachers. Everyone was absolutely perfect. Could not have been better. All of your bosses – perfect! All of your coworkers and all of your relationships – perfect. Every decision, every choice you have ever made – perfect. You could have chosen differently, and that would have been perfect too.

The truth is that you all are ascended. The only reason you are not experiencing yourself as ascended is because you are looking at things and saying that they are not perfect. We could also say that you are not always feeling as you wish to feel. And that is perfect, but you don't need to continue to suffer in that way. When you are not enjoying how you are feeling, you have a belief that something is not perfect. If you believed that everything was perfect, what would there be but joy and unconditional love. We know that you can't fool yourself. You can't just say that everything is perfect if you don't really believe it. That's why we have the *five-step process* (see p. 230). There are these places where you are holding the story in your brain-mind that everything isn't perfect. You also feel something in your body that isn't pleasant. You wish it wasn't there, and the more you wish it gone, the more it stays. Welcome that feeling and go into it until you experience it as perfect. That is the second step. Then from your heart, choose a new story that you love.

When you hold the intention to see the divinity in each person, you are choosing to see everything as perfect. Decide that everything that happens to you or to anybody else is perfect. As you have this intention you will find some of your experiences transforming, without doing a specific process with them. You might think of one of your parents and realize that if they hadn't been as they were, you wouldn't have accomplished what you did. And what a gift have these changes been for you. There is always a story like that with everything you are holding as not perfect. This perfection is not just an ideal. There is an absolutely traceable perfection where everything is connected to everything. You can't tweak things to this level of perfection because your brain-mind doesn't understand enough to know how to do it. Simply accept things as they are and let Spirit do the tweaking for you, trusting that the perfect thing is always happening. You may know what you want, but you have no idea how to get there. Spirit will direct you. You came in with a pre-planning. Before your birth, you said that this is what you want to accomplish in this incarnation. You chose the perfect parents as well as a cast of others to push you in that direction. It doesn't matter whether you were moved by them, or moved in reaction to them.

As you have the intention to see divinity in everyone and per-fection in every action or event that happens, you will have less draw over time to do the *five-step process*. Your body will feel more in balance. In the meantime, the process is a very fast and efficient way to deal with a situation that is difficult for you to perceive as perfect. It helps you to transform your judgment. To accelerate the process even more, have the intention to see perfection in everything and divinity in everyone. The truth is that you are ascended. You have given that intention, not only in your pre-planning, but now consciously. Because you are divine, it can be no other way. As a divine soul, you know no boundaries of time or space. You have always been and always will be. You simply are. You are a being of unconditional love and unlimited creativity. Yes, you.

If you are having difficulty seeing the perfection of something, ask Spirit for support. The understanding will come. You will find yourself increasingly inhabiting a place where your belly-mind is able to accept the perfection of what has occurred, even though your brain-mind may not understand. You accept that it is perfect although you don't yet know why, but trusting that sooner or later you will understand. You ask to enjoy the perfection while the understanding is on its way. Practice looking at the past and find those things that you can now see as perfect, though at the time you were unable to. Everything that has happened in your life has happened for the purpose of helping you to realize your divinity. You were born divine. You have always been divine. But you haven't yet had the pleasure of fully experiencing your divinity. You have felt it in smaller ways. The ways are going to be growing larger. You will look in the mirror one day and from the bottom of your heart say, "I am divine. I am perfect." It's true.

God Blesses You,

Sanhia

How can I reduce stress in my life?

When you don't see perfection in everything that is happening around you, or when you don't experience the divinity in yourself and others, you may think that you have to fix things. You often feel that the responsibility lies with you and a heavy weight descends upon your shoulders. It seems that you must deal with all of these challenges and with the "idiots" surrounding you. It appears that you have to protect yourself from the latter, avoid them, or attempt to control them, so that they don't ruin this great effort you are making to create perfection. It sounds like a tough job. I'm glad I don't have to take that one on.

Your life becomes such a struggle that you lose sight of how total, constant, and unending the battle is. You try to reduce the amounts of stress you are aware of to a level that is bearable, but no matter how much you are able to alleviate situations, life remains a battle. This struggle is your creation. You are choosing to have hell on earth. No matter how much you let go of, the inferno remains. The questions is, "Why are you creating hell on earth to begin with?" You can see divinity and perfection, or you can choose to fight. We have spent the past two messages focusing on the former, so let's try working from another side this time. You don't have to see the divinity in another, when they seem to act as your trigger. Nor do you have to see the perfection of what is happening, to give up your resistance. Just say NO to struggle. Decide to stop fighting. Let go of it. Decide that there is nothing that is so important that it requires straining.

If today were the last day you were going to be in this body, would you spend it in struggle and stress over little things? This is one acid test to see if struggle is involved in your day. Ease up on yourself. As you become aware that you are struggling, take a deep breath and relax. Go do something that does not feel like struggle, something that feels like fun, or joy, or even ecstasy. What would you truly rather be doing right now?

Buried deep in your consciousness is the belief that your very existence depends upon struggle, that if you don't fight to survive you will simply go down – for the third time. And that's it. Your whole life is defined by separation from divinity. Your brain-mind is full of reasons why you have stress. Things have to be done, it argues. This is a story of separation from the divine, a belief in your weakness. Argue for your limitations and they are yours. You are that powerful. The ego arguments for struggle are very rational to your brain-mind. There is no end of them. You will carry them to your grave. Or, you can just say NO. You can refuse to listen to them. You can change your mind. This might throw you into such terror that it will be best to do the *five-step process* (see p. 230). Eventually, you will be able to choose your passions over your guilt and fear with greater ease. The first step, as always, is to have the intention to give up the fight. Remember that what you are fighting against is always an illusion. It is never the truth.

There are two primary places where you can get stuck. One is the belief that the nature of life is simply that you have to struggle. You think you have no choice but to work at something you don't like, that you are required to do all these things you don't want to do merely to survive. If you want to do better than just subsist, it seems you have to strain even more. Look how much hassle is involved just to go have fun on a vacation. The other belief is that anytime somebody else is involved with what you are doing, there will be a battle. You anticipate working together as a challenge and relationships as hard work. That's the story. It is a belief in struggle. You don't have to do it anymore. The battle is totally within you. Nobody else can force you to fight. Every time that you give up a little piece of this resistance you realize a little more of what true joy can be like. If you absolutely give up control, you can sense your divine nature right here, right now.

You have experienced this. You have had moments when you were at peace and your brain-mind was at rest, not wrestling with any devils at all. You were enjoying what was there right then, feeling the unconditional love of the belly-mind. You feel that when you finish the second step of the process.

But you have the story that it is not practical to stay there all of the time. You wonder how you could get anything done, how you could survive. On the other hand, when you believe that there is nothing but struggle, you begin to call for and welcome your death on a subtle level. Nobody wants to live forever if survival means constant stress. Let's talk about what true responsibility is. You are responsible for choosing your reality. You are not responsible for taking whatever steps are necessary for making your reality happen. Spirit does that for you. Let it. There was an advertising program for an American busing company back in the 60's. The image was a powerful, comfortable bus with a competent, professional driver. The voice-over said, "Leave the driving to us." The ad implied that you would enjoy the ride, have fun, relax, be safe and protected, and arrive well rested. In your mind, hear Spirit saying, "Leave the struggle to us."

God Blesses You,

Sanhia

Do you believe in a punishing God?

Let's start by defining mass consciousness. Mass means a large number of people, though not all. Consciousness is the awareness that is in your mind. When you are unconscious of choosing your beliefs, you have surrendered your consciousness to the control of others. The "others" can be called the mass consciousness. In any culture there are a set of beliefs that are held by most people in that society. If you are unconscious, you simply accept those beliefs and they run your life. Though in truth you are divine and powerful, you will manifest according to the illusion of reality of the mass consciousness, and thereby prove its correctness. It is an endless loop. Whatever you believe in, you create. Your ego says, "See. I was right". It is considered blasphemous to oppose the mass consciousness and to proclaim your personal divinity.

Perhaps the cornerstone of the mass consciousness in western society is the belief in a punishing God. Some of you may already be saying, "Oh yes, I was raised with that, but I don't believe in it anymore". My question for you is, "Are you so sure?" Let us start with the first peg. God is unconditionally loving. That is the simple truth. The idea of a punishing God is man-made, not a divine idea. God is unconditionally accepting. There is nothing you could say or do that would be blasphemous to God. Absolutely nothing. The only one who can provide consequences for your words, thoughts, and actions is you. Only you – not God, not other people. If you cannot accept the belief in a loving non-judging God, there is nothing more to say here. You are welcome to follow your life and to make the best that you can of it. However, you would not be here reading this message unless at least a part of you was open to accepting the truth about God. I am speaking to that part of you.

The next step, once you have changed your mind, is to move everything in your body you are holding that doesn't believe in your innocence and your divinity. It is one thing to state the belief – and that does come first – but that is not mission accomplished. It is simply setting a course. The path you are traveling is across what you believe to be your separation from God. If you believe in an angry and judging God, the chasm is uncrossable. How can you approach something that you are terrified of? In that case, you do whatever you can to keep the lion away from you. Your choices include living in the way that you think God wants you to, in order to avoid punishment – or denying the existence of God altogether. Either choice is designed to keep God away, not to bring God closer. That is what keeps you safe, in this illusion of an angry God. Being "good" is a way to deflect God's attention. You also want to hide what you think are your transgressions, both from God and from yourself.

The following step is to realize that that there is no such thing as a sin. There is no such thing as doing something bad that needs punishment. Sin is an illusion of the ego. If there is no judging God, there cannot be sin. You are off the hook. You have the absolute freedom to do anything you want. God will never judge you. This idea of good and bad, and right and wrong, is man-made. This thought can bring a level of terror to you. Because you haven't fully accepted the truth of love as the ruling aspect of the universe, your ego in its fear says that people would be out raping, murdering, stealing, and God knows what else. You are terrified of the chaos that such a world would bring. Take a deep breath and feel that part of you. Ask yourself what part of unconditional love would want to kill or be killed, or to be involved with stealing, raping, or punishing? What part of unconditional love would wish to bring harm to anyone or would deny you whatever it is that you want? What part of unconditional love would create scarcity so you're going to have to fight over what's there?

Whenever these fears arise of what would happen if there were no rules of right and wrong, no judgments, and consequences, they arise out of the belief in a punishing God. If the energy that created you is unconditional love, how could *you* be anything else? How can the creation of a loving God be sinful? You have accepted the mass consciousness that God is angry and judging, and you are punishing yourself before God can get a chance to. You create sickness, financial struggle, relationship problems, victimization, trade-offs, and, finally, death.

First accept a loving God, accept your sinlessness, and give up your guilt. Forgive yourself for everything including your judgment of yourself and of God. Of course, there is truly nothing to forgive. God is not judging, but, because you are, it is a helpful step to take. Since you believe there is something to forgive, continue forgiving until you realize there is nothing to forgive. We would improvise slightly on the maxim "To err is human, to forgive is divine", changing it to "To believe in error is human, to forgive is divine". We could say that the state of divinity is the state of constant forgiveness. Forgiveness becomes acceptance.

Now we come to the place where we arrive in every message. If you are trying to work through all of this with your brain-mind only, you are still holding on to mass consciousness energy. Your brain-mind does not have the ability to let it all go. At best, it can convince you that you can experience your divinity and that God might not be punishing. You will still draw in the illusion of punishment, because deep within your body you still hold the belief in a punishing God. One way to move this is by giving it to your belly-mind by doing the *five-step process* (see p. 230). There is no should, or right or wrong, about doing this. Use any other technique that leaves you experiencing unconditional love. There does not need to be a great deal of struggle in whatever procedure you use. To use no method delays your experience of unconditional love. You deserve to feel unconditionally loved all of the time. Whenever the feelings of fear are felt in your body, go to the website and listen to the recording at www.channelswithoutborders.com/5-step-process/. Allow yourself to be guided through the process. You can also lead yourself through it or ask the support of a friend. Transform that fear into the love that is truly you. When you do the *five-step process* you are allowing yourself to fully feel the unconditional love of God, instead of the judgment and struggle of the ego. I will end by giving you my judgment of you. You are divine. You are loved, unconditionally. Always. No matter what you say, no matter what you think, no matter what you do. Your birthright is unconditional love.

God Blesses You,

Sanhia

What is a spiritual response to a world crisis?

As you are working with your own spiritual healing, realizing your personal ascension, and perhaps using the *five-step process* (see p. 230), there often seems to be a stark contrast between the spiritual work you are doing and what seems to be the "reality" the world is presenting you with. One of the current "realities" is connected to the situation in Syria. This appears to be a complex political situation. The Mideast was destabilized by the Afghani and Iraqi wars instigated by the United States. This led to the formation of terrorist groups in the former Iraq. These groups spilled over the border into Syria. The long-standing dictatorship in Syria began to experience a civil war. Of the groups opposing the regime, ISIS emerged as the strongest. For those of you who are intent on rescuing to make the world a better place and to supporting the "good guys", it is hard to find a champion. In addition, an extremely large number of Syrians have felt that there was no choice for them, in order to protect themselves and their families, but to flee the country and to seek refuge elsewhere. Many of them have fled to Europe, because there were few good options in the Middle East. That is the stage that has been set.

The situation tends to trigger extreme reactions for some people. One response is, "How can we take care of all of these people? We have our own problems. We don't want to accept more Muslims in our country because their ways and beliefs are so different. We would have to take care of them, which is expensive, and they don't want to follow our laws or respect our way of life." On the other hand are those who say, "Oh, these poor people. We have to do everything that we can to provide them with a safe haven, to help them to get there, and to assist them in starting their new lives." Oh, and another response for many people is one of hopelessness. The inner voices might say, "What can I do? This is all too big for me to make a difference. It just isn't my problem." All of these viewpoints come out of a place of fear. For those who do not want to take on the responsibility of helping there is the fear of lack and the fear of becoming victims to the refugees. For those who want to take care of the refugees there is often guilt, which is a manifestation of fear. It is the belief that you have behaved badly and that you will be punished if you don't somehow make up for it. This all comes out of the illusion that there was a "wrong" and that it, therefore, can be corrected. Hopelessness is the fear that one is powerless. The ultimate fear is of death. You can also reread Message 34 *What are we to do with death?* for help in dealing with this issue.

It is time for us all to take a deep breath and to collectively take a giant step backward. Let's look at this whole situation in a different light. First of all, it is absolutely essential to remember that whatever you see in the world is a projection of your ego. If you see chaos, if you see victims, if you see people who don't deserve help because they are responsible for their own troubles, this is a projection of your ego and how you perceive yourself in the world. The first step to take in healing what feels to be enormous world problems, and specifically the situation in Syria with the refugees, is to look and see where your fear is attached. Take responsibility for it and realize that this is about you, not about them. Looking at the situation with unconditional love, taking full responsibility for your own life, you might consider Syria and say, "My, this is an interesting opportunity for healing that they have chosen for themselves." You would not see victims. You would see powerful children of God who have collectively chosen to create a situation that forces them into enormous change. Such change always leaves wide open the opportunity for healing. In your own life, your greatest opportunities for healing often come in the face of what appears to be adversity.

Deal with your own fear that is triggered, perhaps using the *five-step process*, and see this as an enormous spiritual gift for the Syrian people as well as the people of all the countries that are also deeply affected. Then you can look at these people freed of your judgment, guilt, and the feeling that you have to do something to help. Rather, you can see their divinity and the opportunity they have created. You can go into a place in your heart and see if you are guided to support this healing process in some way. Only from this place of unconditional love and acceptance can you be guided to an action that will truly support the spiritual process of another. Remember that the solution to a problem is never about changing others or changing the outside. It is always about taking responsibility, about looking at the situation and acknowledging, "This is me". The solution lies with healing yourself. If you absolutely succeed in that, your personal ascension will change the world.

This is an enormous challenge. It is one thing to choose to be a monk and to go into solitude to work on your spiritual process. It is another thing to stay in your community, your family, and your work where you are dealing with the energies of others and are exposed to much of what is transpiring in the world. But, this is the challenge that you have chosen, to be in the world but not of it. You might wish to go back and read two messages that dealt with world problems for further support: Message 31 *How can I change the world?* and Message 45 *How do I deal with my environmental fears?* You have created Syria for your own healing. This a great gift and an opportunity for you. We encourage you to make the most of it and to find that unconditional love within you. And to live there.

God Blesses You,

Sanhia

How do I deal with the religious conflict in the Middle East?

We would like to further develop the previous message, *What is a spiritual response to a world crisis?*, beginning with the history of conflict in the area called the Middle East and how it ties in with religion, particularly the three major monotheistic ones: Christianity, Islam, and Judaism. The story begins with the oldest of the three, Judaism, and the tale, as told in the Old Testament, of Abraham. He was told to take his people to the land that is now Israel, and to begin a new religion that honored the one God. This land was not empty. From the outset we had somebody guided for religious reasons to take over a land that belonged to someone else. This Jewish god demanded obedience; there were severe consequences for breaking his laws. Years later, the story tells us, the Hebrews left and went to Egypt where they became enslaved, then, following generations of captivity, broke free behind Moses' leadership. Forty years after this, they returned to the "Promised Land" and, again, other people were living there. In the name of god, they fought for and won this land. Over the next 1200 years there was a nearly constant state of war with other religions, mostly not monotheistic, for control of this land.

At times the Jews lost control and were subjugated. This was the case when Jesus was born, with the Romans controlling this land. Jesus was a Jew, we could say a rabbi, and not a Christian. He did not start a religion. But many who were not Jews began to follow some of his ideas, primarily through the influence of Paul. Thus, began the religion called Christianity, which was only loosely based on the words of Jesus. The half of his sayings that were eliminated were partially replaced by the inclusion of Old Testament, or Jewish beliefs. However, the wisdom of Jesus had little to do with the Ten Commandments or the idea of a "chosen people". Jesus's message was simply one of unconditional love and of personal divinity, that held everyone as divine. You love your enemy, because in truth you have no enemy. His teaching was at one with my teaching, as he was my teacher. However, historically, Christianity became the wolf in sheep's clothing. The unconditional love and acceptance of Jesus transformed into a pattern of war and conquest.

Along came Mohammad and Islam, also tracing their roots to Judaism. Jesus was held as a prophet, but not as the son of God. On the one hand they were right; there is nothing special about Jesus over anyone else. What they missed, as did the Jews and the Christians, is that everyone else is as special as Jesus, that we are all sons and daughters of God. So, you had three different groups claiming to have the true knowledge of God, asserting ownership to the heart of their religion, Jerusalem. Over the years there has been a constant conflict over "the Holy Land". When we talk about this dispute, we are not talking about all Jews, all Christians, and all Muslims. The clash is between those who could be called the fundamentalists of their respective religions. Fundamentalism results when fear is the basis of religious belief, rather than love. They are afraid of God and prostrate themselves before the divine. They do not respect themselves or see that they can find the truth within. Fundamentalists go to the sacred texts and claim them to be direct revelations of the thoughts of God. They try to find in the text the truth of what God wants them to do. They have the fear that the failure to do God's bidding will bring His judgment down upon them.

Today, Jewish fundamentalism is responsible for many of the policies of the Israeli government and its refusal to provide a home for Islam in the Holy Land. Islamic fundamentalism is responsible for terrorism in the Middle East and elsewhere in the world. Christian fundamentalism, which has a particularly strong influence on the government of the United States, accepts neither Judaism nor Islam as true religions. Even in Europe are found judgments about Islam and Judaism, seeing the former as intolerant and terroristic, and the latter as controlling international money. That is the situation as it appears to exist today.

I am speaking to you as neither a Jew, a Muslim, nor a Christian, but as a divine child of God, because that is all there is. If you look at these three religions, you will find that the majority of their followers are not fundamentalists. They are trying to find a place of unconditional love and acceptance through the tenets of their religion. They want people to take care of each other. We have just heard the Pope come to the United States with a message to share the wealth, to work to end the vast differences between the haves and the have-nots. This has always been the message of Muhammad, as it has been a tradition within Judaism.

All of this comes back around to and hinges on the teachings of Jesus. Yes, Jesus said to take care of the poor, but his deepest message is the one that is the key to the whole situation in the Middle East. This was to love your enemy, and in fact to see, in truth, that you have no enemy. He was talking about the concept of the "mirror" as I have shared with you on many occasions. What you judge in another is what you judge in yourself. It can be no other way. To bring peace to the Middle East you first find it in your heart to love every single person there unconditionally. Let go of your judgment. Let go of your belief that any child of God could be a victim – not the refugees, not those who are imprisoned or tortured or murdered, not those soldiers who have been physically or emotionally damaged. There are no victims here. The way you care for people is by seeing the divinity in them. When you see their divinity, you cannot see them as a victim. You don't have to travel to the Middle East to accomplish this peace. At the same time, as you hold on to your judgments, you are feeding the fire there.

Drop all stereotyping. If you notice that you are having thoughts about a person because of their religion, let them go. Let your thoughts be about the individual, rather than the group they represent. Then, look into that individual's heart and see who he or she is as a unique child of God. If you find that there is a part that you have difficulty loving unconditionally, that is the part of yourself that you judge. Do the work on yourself, not on them. This is how you bring peace to the world. You don't have to leave your own living room. It is not about arguing with others or convincing them. If you hear prejudicial statements, notice if they upset you. If they do, the healing is to take place within you, not within the other. Use some process to move the energy. It can be the *five-step process* (see p. 230), Ho'oponopono, *A Course in Miracles*, or whatever works for you. There is no one way. The belief that there is one way leads to fundamentalism. If you think that your spiritual techniques are superior, you are feeding the flames in the Middle East. It is okay. All on earth is illusion anyway. However, you will not experience your own ascension while holding feelings of superiority or inferiority.

Remember that it isn't real. In the atrocities that you hear or read about, no souls were injured in the production of that movie. These are all divine, immortal, eternal children of God. There is no damage. The part of you that feels that there was damage is the place to begin your healing. It is the place within you that doubts your own divinity and what Jesus taught when he said, "This and more you shall do". This and more than what Jesus did. Let the peace begin with you. Know that it is all perfect. It is all as it should be, exactly what you need in order to experience your personal divinity.

God Blesses You,

Sanhia

How should I celebrate Christmas?

I would like to talk about Christmas. This is the most important holiday in the western world. That is a confusing thing for some people, perhaps for many. Christmas is supposed to be a celebration of the birth of Jesus. However, Jesus was a Pisces and was born in March of 4 BC. Yes, that's right. He was born four years "Before Christ". The Christian religion, however, chose December to celebrate Jesus's birth. We want to state very clearly that Jesus had nothing whatsoever to do with the establishment of Christianity. We'll discuss more about that, later. The reason the holiday is observed in December is that as Christianity was developing and spreading in Europe, one of the most significant existing festivals had to do with the return of the light. This was more important in ancient agrarian times than it is today. Now you can always go to the store or open the refrigerator to find food. In those days there was only what had been saved from the previous harvest, along with any successes from hunting. It would be a long time until things, began to grow again in the spring. In December the light was scarce, it was cold, and there was often concern about how long the food would last. The midwinter solstice was the longest night of the year. From then on, the light began to return. This brought about optimism and a revelry. There was fear about the dark and this festival expressed the hope that there would eventually be warmth, then growth and more food. Christianity co-opted this celebration, but chose to keep many of the old elements intact. That is why there are Christmas trees, elfish beings, lights, feasts, and more. That is why we have this holiday.

Let us take a look at Jesus. Certainly, the word Christmas contains" Christ". Whether or not you consider yourself to be a Christian, and whether or not you believe in Jesus's existence or divinity, you are well aware that Jesus is the reason for the holiday. As I have said, Jesus did not begin Christianity, and he would not have done so. The religion is not representative of his teachings. There is a small amount of Jesus that can be found there. If you read through the New Testament and look at the words that are attributed to him, perhaps twenty percent of them are in the ballpark of something he might have said. There are an equal number of things that are absolutely opposed to anything Jesus taught. Absolutely opposed. How do you know which is which? If you read those words – in some Bibles the words attributed to Jesus are in red, like someone has highlighted the juicy parts for you – take a deep breath after each statement and ask yourself if this fills you with feelings of unconditional love and lifts you up. Or, does it cause you to feel guilt or fear? If it does the latter, it is probably not an accurate representation of Jesus's real words. When in doubt, throw it out.

I will tell you what I know about Jesus, both from being his disciple in my lifetime as Thomas and also from what I learned after he was no longer directly in my life (lives). I did write down many of the things that I heard him say. These writings have been referred to as The Gospel of Thomas, which was found in the 1940's along with other ancient scrolls in the Egyptian desert. But, that version is not mine. That transcript had gone through several re-writings. Perhaps half of what is there was close to what I had written. Again, use your own guidance if you read this text. Coming back to Jesus – there are some things to say about him that are absolutely true, and that he said himself. He taught over and over that the way to find heaven was through unconditional love. It was not about doing "right" things over "wrong" things. It was not about judging or being judged. It was about being in a state of love. He also said that he was a child of God, created by God. He said that we were just the same as him, that we are no different. He was to us as an older brother, with more experience and wisdom, who was further along the path. Jesus saw the divinity in each person, whether or not the person was capable of recognizing that divinity. He did not teach that there were rules to be followed. He didn't speak of the Ten Commandments. He did not make any statements about what people should do. He did not speak about roles that women should take in society, as opposed to men. He did not differentiate between people based on their religion, sexual orientation, state of servitude, or race. His primary tenets were unconditional love, forgiveness, and the honoring of personal divinity.

That is what can be celebrated at Christmas. It is not about the birth of a savior. Jesus would be the first to tell you that birth was not his beginning. He had always been and always would be, as you have always been and will always be. To make Jesus special, to make Jesus different, would go against the heart of his teaching. He said "this and more you shall do", that is, that whatever he did, we are capable of doing…and more! Make Jesus divine in your thoughts, but not at the cost of denying divinity to yourself. The observance of his birth is the celebration of his divine eternal spirit, which is also the honoring of your divine eternal spirit. It is at this time in the darkness of the year, in the coldness and the unfruitfulness of the season, that it can be helpful to re-affirm your divinity, to hold that light in the dark.

There is no need in your spiritual process to pay any attention to Christmas, whatsoever. It's not necessary. Neither God nor Jesus will frown on you for not honoring the birthday. God does not operate in that way. He honors and celebrates whatever you choose to do and loves you without conditions, as does Jesus. It is for you with your inner guidance, to decide what to do with this day, if anything. But if you are thinking about Christmas, you can use the moment to align yourself with your brother, Jesus, remembering that he holds you always as his equal. His coming was not as a sacrifice, but was as an expression of love. Not only did he not die for your sins, he didn't recognize your sins. Only you hold on to the energy of that. This can be a wonderful time to light a candle and to see the purity and the brilliance of the light that is you. Or find it in the fire you may be sitting before for warmth. For those of you who find yourself in the southern hemisphere, this celebration might feel more appropriate for you in June, in the dark of your year. However, the memorialization can happen at any time, in any month, or not at all. Follow your own heart. You can celebrate your eternal flame at any time.

God Blesses You,

Sanhia

What do you mean by my "old story"?

For some of you there has been some confusion over the <u>first step</u> of the *five-step process* (see p. 230), misunderstanding the meaning of your "old story". Your ego tells you stories all of the time about your experiences and what they mean. For example, your brain-mind might say, "I am really good at athletics", or "I am a good problem solver", or on the other hand, "I just don't get along with the opposite sex; I don't know how to talk with them", or "I never have enough money". As you repeat some of these tales, they fill you with confidence and power. Relating other narratives may leave you feeling uneasy or even terrible. There is a sense of "that's my story and I'm stuck with it". These are the "old stories" that we are talking about, the ones that bring you discomfort, the ones that hurt. We call it a story because it is something you have made up. It's not the truth. Anything that is not about unconditional love, joy, and passion is false. It is an illusion. Today we will talk about these "old stories".

You don't have to live with them anymore. You may not want to hear this, but you are living with these old tales because you are choosing to do so. Nobody is forcing them upon you, though your narrative may state that others are, indeed, forcing your story upon you. If your account is, "this isn't my story, this is just the way the world is," you are denying your divinity. You are pretending that someone or something else is running your life. As long as you hold on to that fantasy, it will be true for you. My job is not to tell you to change your perception. That's your job. I am simply here to tell you that there is no story you are stuck with. That is the simple truth. Let me retract that. <u>There is one story you are stuck with.</u> *You are the divine, innocent child of God. You are all powerful. Everything in this world is your creation.* You are stuck with that. You can deny it, but you can't get rid of that story. It is the only statement that is absolutely true. All of the others are optional; they are whatever you want to choose.

You can hold on to painful stories as long as you wish to, but I encourage you to remind yourself of your divinity regularly, daily. Emphasize to yourself that you are the loving, infinite, immortal power behind everything in your life, even though your ego may be screaming out "I don't believe that; I'm not all of that!" Remember that God loves and blesses you always, no matter what you do. Replace the story of the punishing God with one of a loving God. Let that be your daily focus.

For now, we want to direct our energy toward dealing with these "old stories". They are simply things that happen in your life that cause you pain. It may be that you are not fully conscious of having a story. It might just feel like your experience. Something happened in your life and it hurt. You can feel where you are carrying that pain in your body, both when the event happened and when you recall it to your memory. That is an "old story". That is what we are talking about transforming through the use of *Spiritual Alchemy*. The *five-step process* will only work well if you decide that you don't want the story anymore. You may have an unpleasant "old story" that you are not ready to let go of. That's fine. Hold on to it as long as you wish. But, if you are ready to let go of what is painful in your life, you can do that. Be honest with yourself. Either way the story is serving you. You are not a victim. If you are ready, you can do the process.

There is something else I would like to say about this process of letting go of the "old story". It is a habit to play your tale over and over in your head or through sharing it with others. Every time you revisit the "old story", you give it energy; you feed it. It lives and it continues. If you have done the process and the story comes back, likely, there is another level of the energy to be transformed. Acknowledge it and redo the process. You don't always get every bit of it at once. You transmute what you are able to each time. Eventually, the pain will all be gone from your body. Remember that you are not chasing the fear away, you are transforming it into love. Meanwhile the fear affects you on every level. Eventually it kills you. You leave and come back and do it again with a new plan. When you have made the decision to let go of the "old story", really let it go. If the story comes back, repeat the process. To repeat the tale is to hold onto it. The only catharsis that comes from the retelling is to feel the pain that you are carrying, so that you can focus on it while doing the process.

Otherwise, do not give attention to the story either mentally or verbally. Your story is fed when you receive pity from others. It can be a helpful self-discipline to simply stop. See what happens. Replace the "old story" with your divine story. Ask yourself how a divine child of God would react in your situation. In each moment you are choosing whether to feed love or fear. Be vigilant in noticing which you are giving life to. Don't allow yourself to focus your mental energy on the ego's fear.

You are love and you are loved. Keep your focus there. Step by step you are moving toward the full realization of your divinity. You will get there. That is a given. The *five-step process* merely accelerates the movement. Alleviating the suffering now; that is a choice. God only sees your divinity. Everything in this world is your creation. We encourage you to take your power and to use it, inspired by the love that you are. Have a wonderful now.

God Blesses You,

Sanhia

Why is it hard to let go of victimhood?

In the last message, we talked about recognizing your "old story" and choosing to let it go. But, you really have to want to let it go, and you don't always want to do that. Sometimes, things have to get so bad that there isn't anything else to do but to let the "old story" go. I am a believer in the idea that the least pain brings the greatest gain. You don't have to really suffer to grow spiritually. If you are proactive and get out in front of things, you can choose to have your spiritual progress be as painless as possible. That part of you that we call the ego – the division that doesn't believe in your divinity, thinks you are separate from God, and believes you are going to be punished for this separation – wants you to hold on to the victimization. It seems safer. You have to remember that the ego isn't safe; it is absolutely crazy. It believes in insanity. And it draws immense pain and suffering to you.

I want to talk about how this operates for you. The ego says to fear punishment by God for being guilty. So, there is a hesitation to ever admit guilt. The ego tells you that to admit guilt is to invite the inevitable punishment. What you do then, is to project. Why is your life not working? Why are you upset today? Why are there problems? Because he did this. Because she did that. Because of the government. Because of my boss. Because of my parents. There is always a place to put blame. Unfortunately, blaming never helps. The ego claims it is buying time, that it is protecting you. But blaming never brings joy; it never brings peace or a sense of love. It brings feelings of helplessness. Blame leaves you always victim to the whims and the actions of others. Always. That is an illusion, because victimhood is a lie. It is not the truth. You are the creator. You are the divinity. Whatever exists comes from you, even if you are not aware of your part in the manifestation. As long as you pretend to not be responsible for your creations, they will continue to attack you. You will continue to fight them and to suffer.

I think that most of you can recognize yourself here. But some of you also play the game of "Woe is me". You tell yourself that you are so horrible and weak, and you go about accusing yourself instead of blaming others. However, if you look deeply, you will probably find many judgments of others mixed in with the self-blame. The ego thinks that by taking blame it might be able to avoid the wrath of God. But blaming yourself is the same thing as blaming others. It is an illusion; it is a lie. And, it never makes you feel better. It never heals. Remember that in the eyes of God there is no blame, no judgment, and no separation. God sees only your divine nature. For you to experience your divine nature, you must give up all blame and guilt, take full responsibility for everything in your life, and forgive yourself for every judgment you are holding about yourself and others. When you find the going to be tough, that is the place for the *five-step process* (see p. 230).

I began by saying that you must be fully willing to give up your "old story". There is a very good reason, according to the ego, for holding on to this blame/victim pattern. It manifests in a variety of ways, but they all have something in common. To the ego, it feels like there is a lot to lose by giving up victimhood. There is a comforting security blanket in being the helpless victim. This is something you can share with everyone around you. It is said that misery loves company. You go to your friends and you tell your pitiable story.

"Look what _____ did to me".
"Guess what happened to me at _____?".
"You won't believe what this jerk driver did".

It goes on and on, and your friend hugs you and says, "Oh, poor you. I know how that feels". So, you have this great connection and it feels good in the moment. It is a way to immediately sense love coming from others. They support you.

This may be the only way that you know how to feel this love. The glow doesn't last, however. The pain of being a victim remains. If you do decide to let go of your victimhood, there is a fear that others will abandon you. If you stop joining in the game of enabling victimhood, of supporting it in others and allowing others to support it in you, what is left in your relationships? Maybe others will grow angry and judgmental toward you? How will they react if you stop sharing your blame stories? What if you suggest to them that they give up their victimhood and claim their full power? "Who the hell do you think you are?" they might say. There is a tremendous fear of taking your power. The ego judges power. It is terrified of it.

There is a similarity here with the experiences of those who choose to go to Alcoholics Anonymous. In that case, you want to give up an addiction to substances, as opposed to an addiction to blame. You may find that you have to give up many of your friends and relationships, because they only share and support your addiction. You may choose to replace these people with others who are opting to take their own power. A great change may be required. Parents with younger children might have the fear that if they gave up their attachments, they might not be there for their kids. You might lose your marriage, your parents, or your job, along with your friends. You will become a social pariah. The ego does a wonderful job of spreading this kind of terror.

Ultimately it will come down to one question for you. Are you tired of this shit or not? Do you want to hold onto your victimhood and your unhappiness because you have the solace of fellow sufferers? Is that worth it? If the answer is "yes", you will continue with your "old story" until the answer becomes "no". If you want, now, to experience your divinity, feel your power, know only love, peace, and joy – you say "no" to the ego. You choose to let go of all judgment and blame, and refuse to have pain, suffering, and failure be part of your life anymore. Now, you are ready to let go of the old stories. You are willing to transform the fears you have been holding in your body into love. This will take some time, but the rewards will begin to be felt immediately. You don't have to wait until life breaks you. You can be proactive. Choose to listen to the voice of love. You can experience the minimal amount of pain by choosing now. The more completely you commit yourself, the less pain you will feel. When you make this choice for yourself, ask for support from Spirit. It is there always. It always has been there. It has only been waiting for you to ask.

God Blesses You,

Sanhia

How does the ego divide and conquer?

There is a strategy that has been used throughout history by those who seek to take power from others called "divide and conquer". If one can get different groups or individuals to fight among themselves, it becomes easier to take them over. It is when people are united that conquest becomes a larger challenge. The clever conqueror discovers how to sow the seeds of discontent, to get people's fingers pointing in many different directions. Individuals fail to recognize the real source of their difficulties. They think it lies everywhere else. Many politicians have mastered this ability. Divide and conquer. The ego has always used this technique. Where did these controlling leaders learn how to do this? From the ego. Those who seek to dominate others are the highest expression of the ego on the planet, using force and fear to wrest power from others. Of course, no leader can do this without your consent. This kind of power feeds off of fear. Now we want to look at how the ego accomplishes this.

Some of you, in conjunction with the previous two messages, have been working with your "old stories". We have heard wonderful reports about the successes you have had in using the *five-step process* (see p. 230) with them. Some of you have realized that you hadn't previously made the decision to really let go of the "old story", and decided that it was now time to do so. Now we want to take it to another level. What the ego will often do is let you go off trying to change a story and therefore claim your power and your divinity. But, before you fully achieve success with that issue, the ego taps you on the shoulder and points out another issue which you need to heal. You drop the first issue and go to the second. Then the ego taps you on the other shoulder and points out a third issue, and another, and another, and so on. You are left exhausted and hopeless. There are so many issues to heal. How can you ever get to all of them? Before you can put out the first fire, there is another fire calling for your attention. What to do? You throw up your hands. After a time, you probably find the energy to tackle another "old story", but the same cycle continues. You melt into a puddle of helplessness. Divide and conquer. The ego wins.

Once you are conscious of your divine nature, the ego has to step up its game. Your full embrace of your divinity is the death knell for the ego. This awareness of your divinity will lead inevitably to full realization and your ascension; however long it might appear to take. Being alert to the ego's techniques allows you to minimize that expanse of time. Being mindful to how the ego works will lower your susceptibility to the divisions it is provoking. You begin to understand the ego's game which is intended to keep you in this endless cycle of victimhood and powerlessness.

What we are going to suggest as means for ending this seemingly unending division is that you choose just one "old story". We don't suggest that just any story will do, but that you choose the one that appears to you to be the largest, the most insurmountable. Choose your greatest challenge, the one you feel would be the hardest thing for you to achieve. The truth is that there is no order of difficulty, but the ego is telling you that this one challenge is greater than all the others. The ego tells you that this one is too hard and that you should go for something more easily achievable. Even when you make this choice, you can be sure that the ego will remind you of the roads you haven't chosen. Don't listen. This choice will be easier, because you know that you have taken on a big challenge. Likely, the other baits the ego tries to tempt you with are nested within this larger challenge. If the ego, in its desperation, should tempt you with an even larger challenge, you might, choose to let go of the one you have in favor of the new, seemingly bigger story. If this should be the case, you still are left dealing with only one story, and you can thank the ego for its helpful diligence. The ego will sometimes shoot itself in the foot in order to get what it wants. Ultimately, the biggest "old story" is all inclusive. Don't worry about finding it; let it find you.

Your job is to choose the major story that you are aware of and willing to release. Use the *five-step process* or whatever other technique you might have to transform that "old story" into one of divinity, power, and love. Give it attention every day.

Do this by focusing on your new story, chosen in the fourth step of the process, holding that in the forefront of your consciousness throughout the day. If you should notice pieces of the "old story" creeping back into your consciousness in the form of little fears or guilts nibbling at the edges of your new story, redo the *five-step process*. Do so every day if necessary. When you are working with the second step, and you have felt the energy transform and have moved it to your heart chakra, try doing a full body scan from the top of your head to the bottom of your feet to see if there is any other place where you are feeling discomfort. If you detect any imbalances, work with those spots until you notice no further distress. You might wish to continue doing scans until everything feels clear. Then, it is time to release the energy from your heart chakra.

Feel the simplicity of having just one story to deal with. You may reach a point where you feel that you have fully left the "old story" behind. Congratulations! Now, what is the biggest "old story" you want to transform? Notice that you are not simply jumping from one story to another. It is not an example of divide and conquer. You are simply "trading up". Eventually the *new* "old story" will be the one that is truly all encompassing. You will stay with that story until you realize your ascension. Remember always, that you don't escape your fear by running away from it or by closing your eyes and making affirmations. You deal with your fear by confronting the terror and diving right into it. The ego may tell you to run away, but turn around and face your darkness. Know that Spirit and love are always with you. You will meet them at the heart of darkness. Have a wonderfully focused time with your new story.

God Blesses You,

Sanhia

How do my home and relationships affect my intention to ascend?

We talked several years ago about home and having a sense of home (Message 32). I encourage you to reread that message, but we are going to talk a little differently about home today. We have also talked about relationships before (Message 30). Again, you may wish to review that subject, but we will go in another direction with the information today. Finally, we previously talked about intention (Message 51), and of course you are invited to revisit that correspondence – in fact, it would probably be the most supportive of the three in fully receiving today's communication. We are going to weave these three topics together for you.

Everything always begins with intention. Everything. If you do not express clear intent, you, by default, give your life over to the mass consciousness and to the confusion brought forth from your past lives. When you have the goal to experience ascension, the only thing between you and the full realization of your divinity is the illusion of time. That could involve lifetimes, but it will happen. Much of what we share with you is given with the hope that you might reduce the time it takes you to realize your divinity. Knowing what you want, expressing intention, and making ascension the most important thing in your life – these are the great time reducers. Whatever else you are considering, choices you have before you, confusions you have – ask yourself, "Is this in line with my intention to ascend?"

I want to specifically direct this focus of achieving the realization of your divinity in two ways: first dealing with home, then with relationship. I have mentioned several times about the "mirroring" effect of others. Whenever you are around others, you see yourself reflected in them. Whatever you notice about them shows how you feel about yourself. Your judgments of them are your judgments of yourself. Your love for them is your love for yourself. If you feel yourself to be a victim to them, it is you who have created the attack because of your belief in a need for punishment. As you are conscious of this, you can use it as a healing tool. Your ego does not want to accept these reflections as you. It wants to project on others and to be a righteous martyr. Take this home with you. Work with this within the safety and security of your home. These are frightful things you are encountering. It is a great challenge. It is not easy to fully confront your illusions and your fear, even using the *five-step process* (see p. 230). That's why we encourage you to create a safe home. This is a place where you will have minimal opposition from your mirrors. You will never escape them completely, nor would you want to if your primary intention is to ascend. On the other hand, if you are constantly challenged by your reflections, you go crazy. It's more than you can handle. Create a secure place; I call that home. For some of you this home is the place where you live. But for others your residence is not a shelter. For some of you, home might be a group you get together with, a close friend, or a quiet spot in the woods. That is where you feel protected. The first thing we are suggesting around home is that you make sure you have it somewhere. If your residence doesn't provide such a haven, find someplace else. Look for a space where you feel nurtured and supported in your spiritual process.

If you are in a relationship that doesn't support your spiritual process in a nurturing manner, I ask you what your first priority is? What is your intention? If it is your chosen purpose to become aware of your divinity, living day-to-day intimately with someone who does not reinforce this path makes that realization much more difficult. If this is the case for you, perhaps you have created a safe pocket within your residence. But, still you must venture out into the rest of the house and interact with your partner. The questions are " What are you choosing?" and "Why are you choosing that?" Perhaps your response is to say that you know that your partner is your mirror and so you are using your partner to promote your spiritual growth by taking responsibility when you become upset over what is going on between the two of you. I say that is wonderful, but do you need or want your life to be a constant barrage of perceived attack from your mirror? If you are open and willing to see your fears and what your ego is telling you, there will be plenty of opportunities to experience your ego's voice as you go through your daily life. But, if you are "sleeping with the enemy", it can actually be harder to change your story.

Let's talk further about relationships. Some of you, as you read this, are saying, "What relationship? I wish I had one." If this is your situation ask yourself which is more important to you, realizing your ascension or having a relationship. Be honest. If being in a relationship comes first, it is not likely that you will manifest one that supports your spirituality. You will also likely find the relationship to be a co-dependent one, because you may be entering it out of neediness. What other parts of yourself might you be willing to deny to keep your partner from leaving? If you decide to leave, you have to begin the whole process over again. What will make a new relationship any different? I encourage you to be conscious of what you are choosing. Ask yourself what you really want from a relationship. What would leave you unfulfilled if it were not a part of your partnership? If you have expressed your intention to realize your divinity, how can a relationship be fully supportive if it is not based on a mutual desire to experience your divine natures?

If ascension is your highest intention, you might be more strongly supported in it through creating a safe home for yourself, rather focusing on having a relationship. If this leaves you feeling hopeless, then your issue for healing is hopelessness. Create a network of friends or groups that share and support your intention. Choose a home where you can work with your process, deal with your ego, face your fears, and focus on loving yourself and others unconditionally, without having anyone in your face. Also, work with your fear of never finding the right partner. Come up with a new story. What likely happens is that you will create the partner who fully supports you in your ascension process when you don't need that person, when you are already doing that for yourself. If you are looking for a partner to come in and save you in your spiritual process, you are back to a co-dependent situation. Ask Spirit to bring a supportive partner into your life. This partner can magnify the effort you are already making. Nobody ascends alone. We are all connected. You are never alone. When the person is ready, the partner will appear.

Your ultimate relationship is with yourself and with Spirit. Your process is expedited when you are clear about your intention, create a nurturing home, and are uncompromising when it comes to choosing a partner who supports your intention. I am not necessarily suggesting that if your relationship does not feel supportive, you should move out today or have the locks changed. But, it may be time to initiate a different kind of conversation with your partner. See if that mutuality can be found. If your partner is not able to support you – you have a clear choice to make. Remember that your truest partner is Spirit, and Spirit always loves you unconditionally.

God Blesses You,

Sanhia

Can you explain the terms ego and Spirit?

In past messages, we have used the terms "ego" and "Spirit". Perhaps this is a good time to define what we mean by them. Those of you who are or have been working with *A Course in Miracles* may be familiar with how it uses these words. We will treat them in a similar way. We would begin by reminding you of the truth of who you are, of your personal divinity. You are created in the image of God. You are one with God, who loves you unconditionally no matter what you might choose, do, or think. However, the part of you that we call your ego does not believe this or trust it for a minute. Your ego, in fact, is terrified of God and believes that you are separated from Him. It thinks that God is angry with you for this separation and is going to punish you. Your ego's agenda is all about protecting you from God. One of the ways it does this is by punishing you, before God can do it. Another way of dealing with this fear is by trying to be "good" in the attempt to win back God's love. Your ego is absolutely insane. It's crazy. Your ego believes that you have to try to do everything right. You have to eat right, wear the right clothes, meditate in the right way and with the correct frequency, have right thoughts, treat others right, and so on. This comes from the belief that you are separate from God, which you cannot be, never have been, and never will be. It is an absolute impossibility. The nature of who you are is a child of God. You are created by God in His image, and there is nothing you can do about it. But, your ego doesn't believe this. Your ego will do anything to protect you from God.

Your ego is the voice of fear, anger, jealousy, hatred, pain, suffering, doubt, and self-flagellation. None of it has anything to do with God's love. We would put it this way. God simply does not see your illusion of separation that you have created here through your ego. He does not see it. God doesn't see this hell that you have created. He does not even see those moments when this world your ego has made feels blissful, even heavenly. Even the ecstasy you might experience on the physical earth pales in the face of the true joy, love, and creativity that you are. It is but a taste of it. You may have heard that the human mind only uses five or ten percent of its full capacity. What if it worked at 100%? When you experience bliss in your body...enjoying the beauty of the earth, dancing, having sex, eating food, sharing love with another, or whatever the connection might be...you are at best only experiencing 5% of the totality of the absolutely unlimited bliss, joy, and love that you are. Happiness is a very relative term. If you are receiving electric shocks and then they stop, you may feel happy. Happiness can only exist if there is also unhappiness. Divinity is infinite rather than relative. It has no opposite; it is the "is-ness", the truth of who you are. Your ego, meanwhile, is fighting like hell for that 5%, while denying the existence of the 95%.

What is Spirit? Spirit is a little harder thing to put your finger on. It is not physical, nor of the material world. We could call Spirit an intermediary between you and God. Whereas, God does not see this physical-ness, this illusion – in fact you created it so that you could hide here from God – Spirit is able to see it. Spirit is in between; it is absolutely connected and one with God and at the same time can recognize your confusion. You can have a direct communication with Spirit about your inner turmoil which you are unable to have with God, who doesn't recognize anything about you but your divinity. Spirit can enter into your dream and help you transform it. When you ask Spirit for help – some people use the term "pray" – it is the same thing as asking Jesus or any other ascended master for help. The ascended master is a soul like you, but has recognized oneness with Spirit and can act in this realm while also being absolutely connected with God.

Your job becomes very simple. You can listen to your ego or you can listen to Spirit. You can be guided by your ego or you can be guided by Spirit. You make the decision. It takes a very conscious intention to choose Spirit because the world around you tends not to. The world around you will probably reflect that you would be insane to choose Spirit, even the mirror that claims to be religious. What do you do in the face of such overwhelming opposition? First comes the recognition, the knowing of which of the two you are listening to, your ego or Spirit. If any of the qualities above, which were listed at the beginning of the second paragraph, are present – you are listening to your ego. If you are listening to Spirit, the following qualities might be present: first of all, trust, and secondly an absolute integrity (being true to yourself). Your ego wants you to act in a way that is not in line with your true self, out of fear of what might happen if you are true to yourself. The trust and the integrity fit hand in hand. Meanwhile, your ego is warning you of all of the consequences of going down that road. When you are listening to Spirit there is never a competition, never an either/or, never winners and losers. Spirit always speaks with unconditional love, free of judgment. Your ego speaks from fear and always has limits, competition, and the need for protection.

The next question might be, "Okay. I know I am listening to my ego, but how do I stop?" First you set an intention and you invite Spirit in. You ask Spirit to guide your life. After you have done that, there are two main things you can focus on. One is to have a constant awareness of when and how your ego is acting. Ask yourself how Spirit might guide you here. How would Spirit choose? What might Spirit say to you? If an answer doesn't come quickly, ask Spirit to send you support. The second thing is to practice forgiveness. Your ego operates out of guilt. That is its main fuel. Forgiveness destroys guilt. If you could eliminate guilt from your life, your ego would starve to death. It needs your guilt or the guilt of others, which is easy to find. You simply point your finger and say, "It is your fault". But we know that everything you see around you is just your own reflection. It doesn't matter whether you perceive it in yourself or another. Remind yourself that it is an illusion; that person didn't do anything to you. You haven't done anything either. You are all innocent. You forgive both. You constantly search for the guidance of Spirit, and you continuously forgive when you realize your judgment is in the way. A good benchmark for telling whether your judgment is in the way is to see if you have any. If you do, it is in the way. Nothing is too big or too small. Choose Spirit. Ask for support. Forgive. Know that you are always loved at every moment. Know that you do not have to do one thing to deserve that love.

God Blesses You,

Sanhia

What do birthdays and deathdays have in common?

Everyone in your culture consciously embraces the anniversary of the birth, of the entrance into the illusion of physical reality. Your birthday is a big day, one for joyful celebration. It is an event where everyone honors you, perhaps with a party so that people can express their love and appreciation. The deathday is also a date to celebrate. It is an occasion where you focus on the transition of your loved one. It is a time to consider the spiritual gift that arrived for you that day. Whatever is not healed in you about death will come up for you to look upon. It is a moment to ask Spirit to support you in fully opening up to what you are still holding around death: whatever is feeling unhealed, wherever there is still fear or anger, grief or sadness. Feel where that energy is being held in your body and to call on Spirit to help bring about a transformation. You may want to revisit where we talked about death (Message 34).

Your birthday is for celebrating the moment when you jumped in and declared that you were going for the golden ring again. On that date, you took on a physical form in the hopes that you would remember the truth of who you are this time; that you would realize your divinity and experience the oneness while in a body. The deathday, which is always someone else's, is a celebration for one who came in with you to play an important role, joining you in a mutual support to recognize your divinity. Feel gratitude for that, understanding that the death was a part of the gift. The greatest possible benefit that can be garnered from this is the insight that there is no death. Death is an illusion. There is no "life". You do not begin with a birth or end with a death. You are. Birth and death are but mirages. Your single purpose in creating this chimera of "life" is to realize just that; that it is an illusion. This is not real. It is not you. You are divine, eternal, immortal, and limitless. Each death is a gift to help you realize that. The anniversary of the deathday is meant to honor the divinity of that soul. They died so that you could be free of the illusion of death. The ego sees this as "the supreme sacrifice", but nothing was lost here. Those who die, only leave behind the suffering they experienced while having a body. They are free of all of that now. I have used the term "illusion" several times. Your ego has a great resistance to accepting life and the physical world as illusions. The term cannot be overused. Repetition can only help you to let go of your ego's resistance.

When there is still sadness for you around the deathday, the sorrow is a mask for your fear of your own death. If you fully accepted the soul's immortality and you truly loved the individual who has left the body, you would be so happy for them that they are free of suffering. "Rest in peace" you say, and you would really feel that joy. This is not a peace of emptiness or nothingness, which is, perhaps, part of your story and your fear. It is the peace of seeing that this was an illusion, the peace of knowing that the pains and sufferings of this "life" can all be let go. A gift that is there for you in the deathday is you can realize that you don't have to leave your body to let go of the suffering. That is the last recourse. If you can't find a way to transmute the pain while alive, you can always leave your body. There is no judgment about this. If you choose to leave, you will sooner or later choose to return. Eventually you will get it; you'll accept your divinity. But, since you are going to leave behind all of this suffering at some point, there is absolutely no reason to hold on to any of it for another minute. The deathday is there to remind you of that. You can't take it with you. You can't take your pain with you when you die. You can choose to release it now.

Celebrate your own and others' birthdays. Honor your courage in taking on the form of the illusion of physicality. Love your determination to realize your divinity this time, to ascend. Celebrate the deathdays for those that you love. Don't add the intervening years to their age. Don't visualize what they might look like now. This is not a day to hold them in their physical form. It is a time to celebrate their divinity. They are no longer your parent, sibling, partner, child, relative, or friend. They have dropped that role. You are still lovingly connected with them, but now it is with the truth of who they are. Let the illusion of their life go, as they have already done. Practice forgiveness. Go into your body and deal with your pain through the *five-step process* (see p. 230). Ask Spirit for support. Make every day a celebration of eternal life, of the truth of who they are, and of the truth of who you are.

God Blesses You,

Sanhia

How can I deal with my karma?

I don't believe that we have discussed karma in depth in these messages before, though there has been a reference or two. There is a great deal of confusion around karma. In western religions, it is not even talked about, because karma implies past lives. These faiths acknowledge only the existence of the lifetime you are now experiencing. They believe in only one illusion, not in many. It is from Hinduism and Buddhism that we get the belief in reincarnation and the concept of karma. According to these religions you can have both good and bad karma. What you do in this life will affect your next life. If you do something harmful to another, you will suffer for it in your next incarnation. Conversely, if you do good deeds, your reward will come in your next lifetime. A similar belief is held in Christianity, except the reward or punishment is in the afterlife, and it is permanent. The concept of karma is based on judgment of good and bad, followed by the appropriate reward or punishment. For most people, however, the focus with karma is on the negative. You believe that you are suffering now for something you did in a previous embodiment. On top of that, if you do something you judge as bad in this lifetime, you are condemning yourself to being born again, because fresh karma is believed to only affect future lifetimes. Reading between the lines, if you don't lead a perfect life – if you make one mistake – it's all over. You are going to have to come back and try it again, and suffer for it.

We want to look at karma from several different perspectives. The first thing is that karma implies judgment. It suggests there are good and bad actions. Those of you who are on a conscious spiritual path – wishing to experience your ascension – become focused on living a perfect life. "How do I eat right? How do I meditate and pray correctly? Am I doing the right work? How do I take each step flawlessly, so I don't even step on an ant? How do I breathe so consciously I don't even inhale a gnat?" There is an unceasing focus on doing right. All this comes from the ego. The entire interpretation of karma that we have been dealing with up to this point comes from the ego.

It is fear-based. It is this idea that God is going to punish you for what you have done. God is judging everything that you do, so you take over that job.

Let's look at what karma truly is. It has nothing to do with divine judgment. What karma represents is that in a previous life you judged yourself for an action and never fully forgave yourself. It is you who pulled that forward to this lifetime. You are still carrying that judgment with you. When you were doing your pre-life planning, you looked at these accumulated judgments – or karma – which you were holding and asked yourself how you could best set up your new incarnation to support you in forgiving and letting them go. You planned to draw various experiences into your life to trigger those old guilts. Hopefully, they would be brought to your attention and forgiven this time. Karma is simply the measure of what you have not forgiven. It has nothing to do with payback or retribution. It is not a punishment. The reason it feels like punishment is that you have a tendency, as we have previously mentioned, to punish yourself before God does. This is the insanity of the ego, because God loves you unconditionally and has no judgment, no matter what you do.

In this lifetime, you will experience something as being traumatic. Your brain-mind may identify this as karmic payback time. Perhaps you bow your head and willingly take the punishment, believing that you deserve it. It is a beautiful thing to accept and to let go. However, if you surrender in a spirit of having deserved this, you are not completely through with the energy. A part of you will continue to respond out of fear rather than out of love. On the other hand, a full letting go and forgiveness leaves you at a place where you only choose to follow the guidance from Spirit, rather than your sense of right and wrong. You are able to surrender to trust and love, directed only by the oneness of Spirit.

You are susceptible to choosing as you have chosen before. You are likely to listen to ego instead of to Spirit. Karma is simply self-correction. You draw these karmic experiences to give you the opportunity to choose Spirit this time. The more shaken up you are by the karmic experience, the greater the possibility that you might invite Spirit. If you don't, it's all right. Nobody is going to punish you except yourself. You will get chance after chance after chance. When you choose Spirit, karma is dissolved. It is no more, neither past nor present. Whatever "fresh karma" you have accumulated in this lifetime is also dissolved. There is no further balancing to be done. There is no debt to be paid. It is just a question of when you absolutely forgive yourself, when you fully let go of the ego. Doing the *five-step process* (see p. 230) accelerates the release of your ego. The karma you carry is in your body; it is the energy that you work with in the second step. It makes no difference what lifetime or lifetimes the karma is connected to. Either you have it or you don't. When it dissolves, it dissolves for all time.

Karma is not punishment; it is a gift you have offered to yourself. We support you in giving up the struggle. Surrender the idea that it has to be hard. Let go of the thought that you deserve punishment and that pain will cleanse you and make you worthy. You are worthy right now. Ascension is not something you earn. It is simply about loving yourself and everyone else unconditionally. It is about absolutely forgiving yourself and others. In the process of doing that you will come to the realization that there has never been anything to forgive. God does not and never has judged you. He always loves you. Karma is a gift to remind you of where you are not doing that, where you are choosing ego over Spirit. Welcome and embrace your karma. Use it to practice forgiveness and unconditional love. You are forgiven. Go in peace.

God Blesses You,

Sanhia

Why doesn't money feel spiritual to me?

Michael just pointed out to me that we have never directly addressed money in these messages. Ulla says that money seems to be a problem for everybody. It is funny that even though you have largely done away with physical money in your modern economic system, it remains just as big a problem. When we talk about illusion, what better place is there to look than at money? What value does that piece of paper have? You can't eat it or drink it. You can't build a house or take a trip with it. All you can do with it is give it away, or stow it away. Money is an absolute illusion; it has no value in and of itself. Even the coins that once were precious are now made mostly of low cost metals. You often replace money with a little worthless plastic card or even digital numbers in cyberspace. The thing to understand about money in all of its manifestations is that its primary purpose, as is true with absolutely everything else in your life, is to support you in realizing your divinity. You are immortal, divine beings. That is what you came here to realize.

Money is a tool to help you do just that. You may believe that the purpose of money is to help you survive, but your survival is guaranteed. Your ego may scream out that you don't just want to survive, you want to survive and stay in your body. If you think that money is what allows you to stay in the body, and the ego uses the body to stay separate from God and in pain and suffering, then money must be the thing that keeps you trapped in your earthly hell. If we do away with money, can we eliminate pain and suffering? It is not quite that easy. Ask those who have tried to live outside the financial system.

Let us start with looking at the connection of fear with money, the anxiety that there isn't enough. Money is the best way that you know to attract what you desire into your life. Whether you are looking at the basics of food, water, shelter, and clothing, or the extras that seem to make life worth living, there does not appear to be enough money. You may decide to sell yourself out. You may take a job that you probably wouldn't do if fear were not raging in your mind. Some of you have mastered this denial process by finding work that provides some enjoyment and/or pays relatively well, but if you won the lottery, would you wish to continue with your job as it is? For many of you, your story is that your job takes too much time and energy, has too many distasteful qualities, and leaves you with too little money. The choice seems to be between either working harder or being poorer. There may be fear around deservedness, and poverty can be seen as the only route to heaven. Jesus warned us about the spiritual dangers of the love of money. When you place financial success as your most important goal in life, you have chosen a goal that has no value. If you believe that money will bring you happiness, you are deceiving yourself. No matter how much you create, it will not be enough. Which billionaires have said that they have enough and have stopped accumulating wealth (the answer may be those who are beginning to look at their own mortality)? But the deception is equal if you believe that poverty will bring you happiness. Remember that money is pure illusion. What do you value? If your priority in life is to experience your divinity, the purpose of money is to support that happening. Perhaps you wish to attend trainings or workshops, go to retreats, or receive sessions for your spiritual and physical healing. You don't feel that you can afford them, so your spiritual growth feels blocked off. You can't afford to ascend. That is quite a story.

We begin the healing of your relationship with money by reminding you that the dollar, kronor, or other currency is the illusion of all illusions. It is not real, but exists simply as a temporary convenience. It is a bridge. When you can fly, you don't need bridges. Money provides an easy way to exchange. It releases you of the need for barter, where you must find the person who has what you want and also wants what you have. Money provides a basis for trust where you give service one place and receive service in another. Eventually there will be no need for it. Fear of lack requires you to keep score. As you realize that the supply is infinite, the need to keep track disappears. You don't have to wait for the world to get there. You can go there at any time. You can go there now. You cannot experience your divinity while you are carrying fear about money. Is it possible for God to be unable to generate enough? Is there a limit to the creative power of God? If you believe that you cannot generate enough, you have separated yourself from God. You must not be divine. Part of my job is to shake you gently and remind you that you are divine. Listening to your ego is the only thing standing in the way of manifesting whatever you desire in the moment. You choose to pay attention to your ego instead of to Spirit. Your ego says you are undeserving and that there isn't enough to go around. It tells you that wanting more is selfish and takes away from what others can have. It warns you about what God does to selfish people. The way to ascension, according to the ego, is to do without, to be an ascetic. On the flip side, the ego tells you that those who have abundance have sold their soul to the devil, and they will burn in hell forever. You will be rewarded for your suffering.

What a story! When you decide to stop listening to the ego, your experience will change. It probably won't transform all at once, because it is difficult to stop listening to that lie instantly in its entirety. Ask Spirit to come in and guide you to the truth about money and manifestation. The function of money is as a medium of exchange so that you are supported in the moment as you are following your path or doing the service you came here to do. Money is not a diversion for you. You can be fully focused on love and supporting others to realize their divinity, as you realize your own. Do the work of listening to Spirit and letting go of the ego. Keep your eye on the prize. Whatever is essential for today will be there. There is no need to worry about tomorrow, because it never comes. You are always in the now. You are always supported by Spirit. When your fear about money surfaces, use the *five-step process* (see p. 230). Go right into the face of your fear. You will never be able to accumulate enough money to lose the fear. If you are working a job or staying in a relationship because of fear of money, fly into the face of that fear. Staying is a slow death that will not allow you the true happiness of realizing your divinity. If you want to do something that supports your purpose, but worry about not having enough – spend the money. Trust. Do the process. Remember that it is all illusion. It is just a movie. Play the role your heart is set on. God is on your side.

God Blesses You,

Sanhia

Who are you?

When doing numerology readings through Michael, I usually begin by asking those souls, "Who are you?" I ask them to use terms that are always true. After they have finished, I say that there are two ways that I would answer that question for them. The first would be true for any soul that was sitting before me. The second one would be specific just to them. Today, I want to begin by sharing that first truth about who you are that applies to each one of you that is reading this. It is very simple; it won't take long. You are divine. You are a child of God, created in the image of your Creator. This means that you are a being of unconditional love and unlimited creativity. You are. You have always been and you always will be. You are innocent. You are unconditionally loved by God no matter what you might do, say, think, or feel. That is the truth for each one of you. The reason that you have chosen to come into this physical body at this time is to become aware of this truth and to know that it is your essence, thus realizing your divinity. That's the end of the story. Ulla says that it is not that easy, that it is difficult for many people to believe that this is true about themselves. I know that is the case; I have been in your sandals.

There is also the second, personal truth about who you are. I'm not going to spend much time with that right now because I cannot differentiate here the words that apply to each of you individually. *The Love Letter from Your Higher Self,* your numerology chart, presents that information. It tells you two things. On one level, it describes your confusions and challenges that obstruct you temporarily from realizing the absolute truth of who you are. This information helps you to ask Spirit for support in letting go of those blocks. The love letter also talks about the specific gifts that you have to offer to the world, to the whole, to the one. You use these gifts to support others. After you fully realize your ascension, you continue to use these gifts in support of others, as all ascended masters do. We released the *Ascension Numerology* book so that you could access this specific information and work with it yourself.

There is a third sense of self we particularly want to work with today. These are the thoughts you have about who you are that are limiting and will inevitably bring you pain and unhappiness. These restricting definitions of self leave you feeling less than divine. For example, you might identify yourself as a parent, perhaps a good parent. If you hold that image of yourself, what is your value when you don't have children or someone acting out that role with you? What is your worth? What happens when your children grow up? Who are you now? Perhaps you once saw who you were as being a child. You grow up and you still are a child, because that is the part you hold for yourself. Any pattern of behavior that limits how you operate in society denies your divinity. You may distinguish yourself by the type of work that you do. Who are you when you go home? Who are you when you retire? One of the more challenging aspects comes when you label yourself with a larger classification such as, "I am Swedish" or "I am American". Even bigger and more formidable is when you define yourself by your gender: "I am a woman" or "I am a man". What happens when you identify yourself in these ways is that you take on the mass consciousness that goes along with those definitions. If you say "I am a woman", you may take on the consciousness of "I am oppressed", "I am in danger of sexual attack", "I am paid less than I am worth", "I am a victim", "I am angry at men for all of this", "I need a man to take care of me", or "I am helpless". Not all will take on all of this energy, but all will take a part of it. When you combine "I am a woman" with "I am Swedish", another set of self-identifications emerges. Religion (or the absence of it) can throw in another set of variables. And so on.

I wish to remind you that this body is not the truth of who you are. You have in your many previous incarnations had both male and female forms. You have tried all different religions. You have experienced numerous nationalities and races. None of these are you. You are much more than any definition that you can give to yourself other than the one I gave to you in the first paragraph. All these other descriptions limit the truth of who you are. Then you experience lack, pain, and suffering. You encounter guilt and victimhood. When you leave your body through dying, you will realize it was not who you are. You will notice that you are still here but your physicality is not. The challenge is to have that awareness while you are still experiencing yourself being here in a body. It's fine to have it after you leave – and you will – but you will choose to come back into another body to realize it here. This is where you are to experience your divinity. Be aware of these limiting definitions you hold of who you are. What categories do you place yourself in? Each time you notice one, ask Spirit to support you in releasing that story about yourself so that you can align with your divinity. You can also ask Spirit to show how the divine in you would act in your present situation. Otherwise, you are in the knee-jerk response of your limiting story of you, where you seemingly have no choice but to react in ways that do not bring you the love and peace that you desire and that are your birthright. You deserve it all. It is here right now for the taking. Let go of the ego's story of who you are and claim the treasure that Spirit offers. Hold on to that intention and one day it will be yours. The time up until then is an illusion. Your truth, your divinity, is forever.

God Blesses You,

Sanhia

How do I move from a lack of faith to trust?

Trust is having faith that whatever is happening now is perfect. It allows you to be fully present in the now. The ego is not capable of doing this. It either dwells in the past in guilt and blame about what could or should have been, as well as mourning for "the good old days", or it imagines a future – worrying about what might or might not happen, or fantasizing about some dream that it doesn't really expect will manifest. Trust is centered right here, right now. It is aligned with Spirit and, therefore, with God. Trust and faith are interchangeable terms. When you trust absolutely you experience only love; fear is dissolved. When you have faith, you listen to the voice of Spirit within you and follow it without question.

It's easy to discern between the voice of Spirit and the voice of the ego. The voice of the ego always possesses doubt. It fosters worry about what the future will bring based on your current choices and actions. When you have faith, you know that your current action is perfect and whatever you have drawn into your life is exactly what is required. It is not necessary for you to understand why it is perfect. That information will come when the time is right. Faith is never dependent on proof, which is a demand from the ego. Proof is really saying, "I cannot trust Spirit until you can absolutely show me that Spirit is trustworthy". This is a demand that can never be satisfied. Trust cannot be earned. When you do not trust Spirit, you are merely projecting your lack of faith in yourself. You don't trust your intuitive process. You feel separate from God and do not believe a direct contact is possible. Perhaps, you want a "burning bush" experience, or something like what Gary Renard manifested with Pursah and Arten, as he related in *The Disappearance of the Universe*. You want Spirit to create something that appears to be outside of you, to speak to you. You want a miracle. If you were to manifest such a miraculous event, over time you would likely come to doubt your experience and go back to your old ways. Trust is to be found within you.

How do you move from a lack of faith to trust? The first step always is intention. You decide that you want faith, that you wish to trust in Spirit. You ask for faith before you have certainty that there is something to believe in. Your ego will resist your attempts at faith at every turn. A strong declaration of your intention to have faith helps you bypass the ego. Maybe your lack of faith hasn't created enough discomfort for you yet. Perhaps things have to get a little worse. Possibly you may have to bottom out so that you have nothing left to lose. Or, you can shorten the time of pain and suffering by asking to trust now. As soon as you make the request, Spirit will begin sending faith to you. The only reason that you don't fully trust now is because the ego has set up blocks to keep that from happening. It believes that God cannot be depended upon. The ego thinks that God is out to get you, and therefore it needs to protect you from Him. But, when you don't trust God, you don't trust yourself – you and God are one. This becomes a dead end, where your life is filled with mistrust.

After giving your intention, the second step is to listen. When you find yourself at a point where you are worried and fearful about what will happen, and don't know what to do – ask Spirit for direction. And listen. Trust what you hear. The ego will want to doubt and question, perhaps even to deny that there was a response. But Spirit always answers. Trust the first thing that comes. Act on it. As you respond to the guidance you receive, future directives become stronger and clearer. Your action is a demonstration of faith. Trust is beginning to grow within you. This faith will continue to expand as you feed it. You feed it by going inside and asking Spirit for support, whether you call that meditation, reflection, or prayer. You listen, receive a message, give thanks, and act. And your faith increases. You can also develop your faith by expressing gratitude toward everything that you have in your life, seeing it all as a gift from Spirit. If you are struggling to see something as being a gift, ask Spirit to help guide you to acceptance. The truth is that it can only be a gift; you are always connected to God, and God only sends you his loving grace. Because you are reading this, I know that you have already decided to welcome Spirit into your life. You have already chosen to become aware of your divinity. Even if the commitment is not yet strong, it is there and it is increasing.

What you feed in your life grows. If you trust Spirit, it will flourish in you. If you feed the ego by giving power to its doubts and fears, it will swell. And let's face it. The ego doesn't need any more help. It has been running this show for lifetimes. It's time to give trust a chance. When you have faith, you are in the realm of peace and love. That state continues to strengthen until nothing can shake it. All you are asked to sacrifice is your doubt and your fear. Doubt and fear can only manifest more doubt and fear. This will be your fate forever until you choose to trust, which will happen sooner or later. It doesn't matter if you wait. The illusion will wait with you. It's not real. It's not going to do you any true harm. I have faith that you will eventually choose to trust Spirit. Why not do that now? I know that the choice of trust leaves you absolutely safe. In fact, you are always safe. But if you listen to the ego, you will never experience a *feeling* of safety. Whatever you choose.

God Blesses You,

Sanhia

What can I do with the fear I feel over Trump's election?

As some of you may be aware, there was a presidential election this past month (November 2016) in the United States. Oh! You are all aware of it. Okay. How many of you were pleased and excited with the results? I don't hear anyone cheering. How many of you were terrified by the results? Wonderful! You see, fear is what this election was all about. It was a thumbs up or thumbs down vote about fear. If your reaction was fearful, you were part of the thumbs up vote. You voted (or didn't vote) out of fear. You have helped to create this election result. I say this not as an accusation, but as an encouragement to take responsibility for your creations. Fortunately, it is all an illusion... or we might all be terrified now. I'm not. I feel fine. There is only one reason why you are here now in a physical body on the planet Earth and that is to realize your divinity – to know that you are one with each other and with the creator God. He doesn't care who is president of the United States. It doesn't make any difference. If it makes a difference to you, you have given your power away. You are claiming to be a victim of outer circumstances, or are perceiving others to be caught in the cross-hairs. Either way it is a projection of your own fear.

The reason for voting at all is simply to select the candidates who most embody the love that you have in you, that most suggest that the loving, trusting, divine energy that is the truth of you will be expressed and shared with others. Whether or not the president of the United States seems to embody that energy makes no difference to you. The question is, "Do you embody that energy?" Are you a being of love, light, and truth or are you a being who is spreading fear and darkness, guilt and blame? It is a very easy choice: love or fear. For those of you who are choosing fear, congratulations. You have elected the perfect leader – even if you did not vote, even if you are not a citizen of the US. The residents of Sweden and other countries feel strongly affected by the election results, also. It is a world event. If you are feeling fear, that is a choice. Nobody is forcing you to be afraid of what will happen because of this election. When you are choosing love, you know there is only perfection, that everything is happening exactly as it should. You trust in what is presented. The plan may not be obvious to you, but that does not mean that it is not present. In the previous message we talked about faith. Faith is where you go forward and act without proof, operating in the trust that divinity, that love is all there is.

How can this election outcome be in service to the planet, when your brain-minds are saying, "No, this is going backwards; this is not going in the right direction"? Yet at the same time, more and more souls on earth are making the conscious intention to realize their divinity. These beings are giving increasing trust to this process. Trust that this election is a part of that continuity. I will tell you a few things to whet your appetite, but ultimately it is you who are to go inside and ask Spirit to help you release your fear about the election and trust in its perfection. One of the ways that the election is serving is that for some of you it is important to see the world improving in certain ways. It is vital that what you see outside match what you want to feel inside. Actually, you have the process reversed. What you see in the world reflects what is going on within you. All we have at this point that we can look at is an election. Some votes were cast and winners were declared. Yet some of you already are rushing ahead and projecting the most horrible things occurring. Does that come from love or fear?

A great gift from this event can be realized because some of you on the spiritual path are looking to be saved. You are hoping for a great leader to come along to rescue you. You will never be saved from the outside. There is nothing there for you to be protected from. The fear is illusory; it is not true. No matter who is in power in the world's governments – what they do or how human bodies are affected – they are absolutely incapable of doing any damage to the truth of you or anyone else. The part of you that doesn't believe that has created this test for yourself. Think back eight years. Remember how excited many of you were at the results of the election that had just happened. What hope you had for the world! How peace would come! How racial equality would be achieved! A whole new period of harmony and love was being ushered in, The Swedish Nobel committee even awarded Obama a prize in anticipation of the great good he would do. Now, eight years later, how did that dream work for you? For many there is a disappointment. Perhaps in eight years you will be disappointed that the Trump presidency was not as bad as you thought it would be. Or would you call that a pleasant surprise?

Now it is time to step up and take control and power over your life. Why give that authority to Donald Trump, especially given what you think he will likely do with it? But why give it to anybody? Except Spirit. Let this election be a great healing gift for you. Give thanks, not only to Donald Trump, but to all those who voted for him as well as those who stayed away from the polls and didn't vote for his opponent. Give thanks to everyone that you judge for the results of this election. Acknowledge them for giving you this golden opportunity to take your power, let go of the belief that you are a victim to outside circumstances, and know that there is only love, only Spirit acting here and everywhere. Nothing else is real. Ask Spirit to support you in realizing this. Forgive Donald Trump and his supporters and the non-voters. Forgive yourself. Forgive, forgive, forgive. Love, love, love. You have a wonderful opportunity here. I encourage you to take it. I encourage you to be open to the possibility of love, and see the divinity in Trump and in yourself. It is you who controls your destiny. Your leaders can neither make you nor break you. Only you get to do that. Give yourself a break. Give yourself a hug.

God Blesses You,

Sanhia

What is the difference between unity and oneness?

On day one of the new year (2017), I have been asked to speak about oneness. Interestingly, the universe is going into a ONE year today (numerologically). See more about the numbers on www.channelswithoutborders.com/the-numbers/. We have talked about the illusion, about this physical world being an illusion. And it is a very convincing one. I want to say that you have done a marvelous job in creating it. It is very believable. But there is one part of this illusion that is particularly hard for me to swallow: that is where you consider yourself to be separate from God, and therefore not to be divine, but to be human with all the baggage that includes. To be human is to be with what Christians call "sin". But even if you don't consider yourself to be Christian, you probably believe that there is such a thing as right and wrong. If you ever judge yourself or another, you believe in sin. If you believe in judgment, you think that it is God that judges you, whether that belief is consciously held or hidden deep within.

Within this story about sin and judgment and guilt is the illusion of separation. That doesn't sound like much fun at all. When you choose divinity, and being one with God, there is nothing but love and joy. That is the divine nature. Why, you might ask, would anyone choose separation, pain, suffering, and guilt instead of love? The short answer to that is that your ego doesn't believe you are divine, and doesn't even believe there is a choice that can be made. The significant questions become, "How do I opt out of this? How do I choose divinity? What is that like? What is it like to be aligned with God?"

Two terms are often used interchangeably: *unity* and *oneness*. Let's investigate what these words really communicate. Unity suggests that two or more are joined together. Because they can join together, they can also separate. You have the example of the United States of America. There are fifty states that have chosen to unite under one central government. Is there oneness? Do all of the citizens feel at one with each other? This is a rhetorical question. In this case, unity and oneness are quite different energies. Unity means to join together while still maintaining a separation. You have two people united in a marriage. Do they become one person? Some would like to hope so. Given the evidence that over half of the marriages end in separation, we would say "no". There was a temporary union, but not a oneness. The truth is not that you are united with God and with each other, but that you are all one. The experience of ascension is the realization of this absolute oneness. Some of you may have had a deep spiritual experience where you have felt this oneness, whether through meditation, a psychedelic drug experience, or simply as a spontaneous happening. What you all have in common, no matter how you have had this experience, is that the feeling of oneness did not last. It eventually disappeared and perhaps you have been seeking to replicate that state ever since. But, it is elusive.

You may ask Spirit to bring you into oneness. More accurately, you can ask Spirit to help you realize your oneness, because oneness is your true nature whether you realize it or not. You don't do something to become one. You don't earn it. You already are and have always been one with God. While you may not be experiencing this oneness right now, you do experience your separation. The separation is an illusion, but it feels very real to you. You encounter separation when you feel attacked by another or when you judge another or yourself. When you attack out of fear you feel separation. When you feel any negative emotion, you are experiencing the sense of separation. The role unity plays for you is to have it as an intention now, when you are feeling this separation. When you forgive another and you forgive yourself over whatever incident is there between you, your intention is to create a unity between the two of you. When you feel afraid that God is judging you, create unity with God through asking for forgiveness. These are steps that your mind can handle, even though it is in separation. You can focus on forgiveness, so there is no feeling of separation between you and your brother or sister, or between you and God. It is easier to focus on unity than on oneness. Ascension is oneness, and that step will come. In the same way, you focus on forgiveness, even though the absolute truth is that there is nothing to forgive, nothing ever. So, there is no need to forgive, but your mind cannot accept that. It is so accustomed to a state of sin and judgment, blame, and right and wrong. All that you can do now is to notice when your mind goes into guilt or judgment and use forgiveness to help establish a unity between you and others. The truth is that you are one, but first you may settle for unity.

Take advantage of the tools you can use. Use the tool of forgiveness. Aim for unity. Choose to end all separation. Do that until the judgment falls away because you realize there is nothing to judge. The separation falls away because you know you are one. It is no longer just an idea or a belief. You know it. The quest for unity and the act of forgiving are your spiritual training wheels. If you keep using them, you will eventually have no use for these aids whatsoever, because you are absolutely aware of your divine nature. Spirit will remove your wheels without even telling you. You will simply find yourself flying freely in your innocence. We will ask you this New Year's Day to begin or to continue to forgive and to seek unity throughout this ONE year. And we wish for you a year of unconditional and unlimited love.

God Blesses You,

Sanhia

Why do I feel abandoned by God?

Some of you have expressed anger to me – perhaps not directed at me, though you may have wanted to shoot the messenger – because of things I have said about God. You feel that God doesn't pay any attention to you, that He is not aware of your struggles and your pain. You feel abandoned because none of this exists for God. I can understand, on one hand, why you might draw that conclusion. I have explained to you that this earthly experience is all an illusion. Nothing in your physical world is real. The only things that truly exist are absolute love and divinity. This illusion you have created in the physical realm of bodies and fear does not exist in the mind of God. He does not see your experience. God sees only the truth in you. He does not see your fantasies of separation, judgment, and pain. He sees your divinity, your holiness. Hearing that causes some of you to feel that God doesn't really care about you. He is just going to let you hang out here in your pain and suffering. All your prayers and cries for help are ignored. To your great surprise, I have a number of things to say about this "abandonment".

If God could see your illusions, it would make them real. Think what that would mean. If your body truly exists; if this earth and universe are existent; if your pain, suffering, and fear are real; they will go on forever. When you die, and leave all of this "reality" behind you, you will realize that none of it was actually taking place. This you realized after your last incarnation, as well as following the multitude of others you have experienced. When you no longer have a body, you still are, just a whole lot lighter without the excess baggage you carry with you now. All of the things that felt so necessary, vital, and important in your physical experience are gone. They are simply gone. If they were real, they would still be there. When you ask God to give them reality, be aware of what you are asking for. You are asking for your hell to be permanent. It is to your saving grace that God does not see your illusion, seeing only the truth of you so that you have the potential of also holding the truth.

Rather than abandoning you, God has sent the Holy Spirit. This is a difficult concept to fully understand. In Christianity, they talk about the trinity of God: Father, Son, and Holy Ghost or Holy Spirit. Usually, even though the concept is alright, the execution of it is woefully inadequate. The Father is often pictured as judgmental and punishing; the Son is limited to Jesus, excluding all of the rest of the Sonship (which includes you and me); and the Holy Spirit is often simply not understood at all. The Father is the originator God – all loving, all powerful, all creative. The Son is you: whoever is reading this; whoever isn't reading this; and whoever has, is, or will be in a body. The Son is created in the image of the Father: divine, all loving, all knowing, all powerful. But, a part of the Sonship has chosen to believe in a separation from the Father and fears retribution for that action. That is the case for all who have chosen human form. God recognizes that you believe yourself to be lost, but does not experience the trauma you have created. You are like a sleeping child experiencing a nightmare. The loving parent recognizes that the child is having a bad dream and knows that it is terrified, but cannot penetrate into the illusion. The parent knows that what is being experienced isn't real and that sooner or later the child will wake up. The parent tries to lovingly awaken the child and to assure it that it is safe. It is the Holy Spirit that carries out this function.

The Holy Spirit is the intermediary between the Father and the sleeping Son. Spirit is designed in such a way that you can ask for Its support, supplicating to be brought into conscious alignment with the Father. I want to remind you that you are not being helped to establish alignment. You are already aligned with the Father. You are one with God. You are one with each other. What is lacking is the awareness of that oneness. This does not take away the truth of who you are, but it does keep you from having the experience of your divinity. Rather than living in the divine love of your birthright, you live in fear. By asking Spirit for support, you can realize your alignment with the Father. The role of the Father is to hold the course, to hold it steady, to hold the truth, to never waiver, and to never give any reality to the hell that you have created. The Father always sees your perfection. It is your role, as the Son, to give up the ego, to stop choosing to listen to it, and to choose divinity. To facilitate your process, God has created the Holy Spirit to help those of you who have chosen ascension, and want to give up fear and illusion. The Holy Spirit is there to give you a helping hand. He is aware of your illusions, but does not take them seriously. Your task is to believe Spirit, rather than the ego. Spirit is there to support you in constantly choosing love over fear.

You can ask God to come down to earth and enter your hell. God won't hear you. Spirit will hear you, however. Even as your faith in trusting Spirit's voice over the ego becomes stronger and stronger, there is still a step between believing and knowing. When you cross that line into knowingness, you no longer feel a need to talk with God, because you are fully aware of your oneness. In the meantime, rest easily in the knowledge that God's love for you is eternal and that dissolution of your hell is a certainty. The consistent message from Spirit is "lighten up, everything is moving forward perfectly".

God Blesses You,

Sanhia

How do I discern Spirit from ego?

We have been encouraging you to choose love over fear, Spirit over the ego. Some of you have asked how to tell the difference. Right now, any decision you make is likely to be fear-based, whether you choose to listen to the ego or to Spirit. If you opt for the ego, you do it out of fear of what might happen to you if you don't follow its direction. When you decide on Spirit, you have the fear "What if this is the wrong thing to do?" The ego is very good at playing that kind of game with you. "Don't you think somebody would have been doing it like that a long time ago if that was the way to do it?" "What if everyone acted that way?" The main message from the ego is that if you don't do as it suggests, something bad will happen to you. You feel that the only safe thing is to do what you don't want to do. When you are listening to Spirit you think "That is what I really want to do, but I'm afraid to". The fear is that you will get hurt by doing what you want to do. Deep inside you can hear what you really want, but you are afraid to act on it. The voice of Spirit is saying "Go for it". To sum it up, the easiest way to discern the two voices if you are doubtful is this: If you follow out of fear, the voice is likely the ego; if you are afraid to follow, the voice is likely Spirit.

Spirit will remind you that if you listen to the voice of the ego only one thing is certain. You will die. Everyone who has done things the ego's way has died. You may be wondering where you find those who have listened to the voice of Spirit. The ego is correct when it tells you that there aren't many. They are called ascended masters. The one you probably know best is Jesus. When you read his channeled message in *A Course in Miracles,* you are getting a training in how to listen to Spirit and leave the voice of the ego behind. The same thing happens when you study these messages. When there are few accompanying you on your voyage, the odds are greater that you might be listening to Spirit.

Mass consciousness is one of the voices of the ego. It takes great courage to choose Spirit over ego. Each of you have come back countless times hoping that you have set things up in such a way that this time you will pick Spirit. From where I sit, it's a done deal. It doesn't matter if you ascend in this body or twenty bodies from now. Nothing will stop you from realizing the truth eventually. You will get there. I have no fear for you. It doesn't matter whether you listen to Spirit now, or not. And so it is with God, who sees only your perfection, only the truth of you. Even now in the midst of your fear, you are absolutely one with God, totally connected. Everything around you is illusory. None of it exists. You can ask God to stop all of this madness, to come down to earth into your hell. God won't hear you. As we mentioned in the last message, while you are in illusion the best you can do is to talk to Spirit. Even when you begin to consistently put your faith in God, in Spirit, and in your divinity, there is still a step between believing and knowing. When you know, you will feel no need to talk to God because you are one. When you ask "Can I talk to God?", you are really saying you want to ask God for help. This is what you do when you pray. You may think your prayer is going to God, but it isn't. It is heard by Spirit. Spirit sends you support to help you to choose the voice of truth.

Let's return to the original question of how to discern the voice of Spirit from that of the ego. Begin, as always, with the intention. Ask Spirit to support you in this goal. Ask for the faith to follow your heart, even when you are experiencing fear and doubt. If the ego wins the battle, let it go. Forgive yourself and try again. The ego might win many battles, but it cannot win the war. Remember how the voice of Spirit feels. When you fully want something to happen from your heart, that is its voice. Remember that the guidance is always for you. Spirit won't tell you how another should act toward you. It is all about you. This illusion is your creation. You can ask Spirit to bring you moral support, but any attempts to make specific people play certain roles for you is always the work of the ego. It begins, always, as a choice to listen to Spirit over the ego. You do it because you believe it is the truest thing to do. Eventually there will be no choice. The only voice you will hear is that of Spirit. I call that ascension.

God Blesses You,

Sanhia

Does love require me to sacrifice?

There is a great confusion that intertwines love and sacrifice. It is this belief that if you love someone or something, you must make sacrifices for them or for it. This belief causes many problems. It is a confusion because love is of Spirit and sacrifice is of the ego. The ego believes that the only way to get something that you want is to give up something that you also want. We can call that a "win-lose" situation.

I want to begin with a short history of this perplexity. Most of you are familiar with the Judeo-Christian story, expressed both in the Old and the New Testaments. Let's start with the Jewish Bible, the Old Testament. It is filled with sacrifice. God, or Yahweh, is constantly demanding something from the "chosen people". Many are animal offerings, but in one particular story we have Abraham, the father of Judaism, being asked to sacrifice his beloved son, Isaac, who had come to him late in life as a reward for his devotion to the one god. Abraham was told to take Isaac up the mountain for this surrender. Reluctantly he agreed. Sacrifice for the love of god. God lets him off the hook at the last moment. The message, however, is that the proof of love is a willingness to make sacrifice. This is found carried forward into Christian belief. There the doctrine is that Jesus gave himself, that god sacrificed his only son, to free us from our sins. Love and sacrifice. I want to remind you that no such thing actually happened with Jesus. There was no sacrifice involved. This was a gift of love freely given from Jesus's heart, following the loving voice of Spirit. If you want to hear the truest expression of Jesus's teachings, I recommend *A Course in Miracles*. If you read the New Testament, I suggest that you limit yourself to the words attributed to Jesus, and still use your discernment (see the previous message).

I want you to know that the god of the Old Testament, who for many is also the god of the New Testament, is really the ego. It is not God. God never asks for sacrifice. How could an all-powerful, all-creative, all-loving God ever have a need that could only be filled by human sacrifice? It makes no sense whatsoever. It is a crazy thought. Sacrifice is an attack, not an expression of love.

When you sacrifice for another, what you are communicating is that that person is not divine. You are affirming their helplessness. Only by the sacrifice of your blood can they survive, be happy, and prosper. What a story! This is an attack. An attack on another is really an attack on yourself. How can someone else not be divine unless you also are not divine? Every sacrifice you make is attack upon yourself.

You don't usually offer blood sacrifices any more, although patriotism may ask that you give your life for your country. While some believe in giving their life for their country, others believe that they must be willing to surrender all to help the oppressed of the world. This is not to suggest that to aid another is an attack. Only when the action is offered in the spirit of sacrifice is it an attack. When you do for another out of the love in your heart, out of divine inspiration, it is not an attack. This is something you truly desire to do. It doesn't matter to you how it is received, whether there is gratitude. It is done out of your joy and freely given.

Look at your relationships, especially your committed relationships. In what ways do you feel that you have to deny yourself in order to maintain a relationship? Or even to have it to begin with? How many women deny their independence, career aspirations, or freedom in order to have a relationship? How many men feel tied down, denying themselves, not allowed to be "real men" anymore because of a relationship? When children come along the feeling of the necessity for sacrifice increases.

The place to begin is by recognizing that sacrifice is not an expression of love, but is an attack. It is a byproduct of guilt. Your ego will tell you that you will lose everything if you do this. This voice will tell you that others are dependent upon your self-denial. Have the intention to stop making sacrifices. Ask Spirit to support you in strengthening your will to give up sacrificing and to always come from love. When the fear comes up – and it will – use the *five-step process* (see p. 230) to help you transform it into love. When you are in a state of unconditional love you can clearly hear Spirit's guidance.

When your ego is telling you that there are others out there depending upon your support, I want to remind you that it is all you. Everything that you see is you. If you perceive neediness that seems to require your sacrifice, that is your neediness. If someone tells you that if you really loved them, you would give them what they demand from you, it is your own ego that is speaking. How long will you believe that you have to thrash your own back in order to become pure enough for God? Sacrifice is self-flagellation. It is an attack upon yourself. This is why some people are terrified by love. The fear is that loving another will call you to a deep painful sacrifice. The only way to be free, in that case, is not to love. What a tangled web the ego weaves. Avoiding love will not bring an awareness of your divinity. If you stop sacrificing, instead committing to love and to transmuting fear into love, you will be able to hear Spirit directing you. This guidance will always lead you into love and out of sacrifice.

This is a great challenge. It is a fearful thing to give up sacrifice. The mass consciousness says that sacrifice might buy you redemption, might bring you forgiveness from God. But, it doesn't work that way. Sacrifice only keeps you separate from God, who requires nothing from you and offers you everything. God only asks you to be your true self. Set yourself free.

God Blesses You,

Sanhia

Did Jesus die for our sins?

The holiday of Easter has just passed; perhaps some of you celebrated it. In the last message, we talked of love and sacrifice. In the world of Christianity, the great story is of the martyrdom of Jesus. That legend has been passed down for 2000 years. As it is told, Jesus, the only Son of God, came down from heaven out of his Father's love for us. God sacrificed his only Son. He did this because we humans are bad. We are sinners; we are evil. The only plan God could come up with to allow us to return to him in heaven to be saved, was through offering the crucifixion of his Son. That is the story, a very sad tale. It is filled with graphic descriptions of suffering, torture, and betrayal. However, this is nothing more than a fairy tale. It is not true. This is not what happened. The true story is that Jesus was not the only Son of God. We are all the Sons of God. He did not come to atone for our sins, because God does not recognize our sins. Only we see our nature as sinful. We see this because we believe that we chose to separate from God. We are terrified of God and fear his vengeance for what we think we did. This is all part of the myth. Jesus came to tell us that it's not true, that God loves us. Absolutely and always. There is nothing we have to do to earn it. It is just for us to realize that we are divine, that we are one with God.

Jesus came to earth of his own choice to save himself. He wanted to become aware of his divinity while in a body. Easter is the celebration of his self-realization. That is what the resurrection was. It does not represent dying and coming back to life again. Death is an illusion. The resurrection represents the "death" of death, the realization that there is only life. There is only life and always life, in divinity. That is the true nature of every soul. Easter is a time to remember this truth and to let go of death, suffering, fear, and the belief that you are an evil sinner.

You may want to ask me why this made-up story has been passed down and believed by so many. There seem to have been eye witnesses. People recorded these happenings. Why would it have been passed on like this? Don't tell us it's a lie Sanhia! Well...this story is like all stories. They are imaginary. No story has happened. Nothing that you attribute to an action by those in human bodies, no none of those stories are real. Nothing has happened in the truth of God. You have manifested this illusion that you have an earth. You create all of the stories that take place on it. You stay in an endless loop with those stories, a seeming infinity of bodies and lifetimes. This goes on until one day you wake up and realize that there is only now, only this moment. There is only the truth, only love. Everything else you have been making up. Meanwhile, because you think you are a sinner you created a savior, since your story says that you can't save yourself. You believe that somebody has to pay for the sins you imagine you have committed, so why not have Jesus do it? He's got big shoulders. He is the Son of God. Let him do it. The problem is that you are still stuck with the guilt. Not only are you a sinner but you let Jesus take the rap for you, leaving you even further away from God (This perhaps is a good thing. Have you noticed how he treats his Son!).

What if we look at the life of Jesus from his perspective? He came in with a high level of knowledge of truth, brought forth from previous lifetimes where he did much work. He created a wonderful support system in his pre-planning. On both sides of his family there were great spiritual workers who came in with him to support his process. His father Joseph ascended before him, showing him the way. When it came time for his full realization, which required an absolute surrender to Spirit, he was told that his path was to go through this "Passion Play" of crucifixion. In this way, the story would be recorded and passed down for the ages. Even though the facts would be grossly incorrect, the seeds of the truth would be there for those who have ears to hear with. It seemed that a trusted associate turned on him. In truth, Jesus asked his good friend Judas to play a role. Judas did not want to carry out that assignment, but Jesus convinced him it was part of Spirit's plan. This was an act of love, not betrayal. Though what people saw at that time did look like punishment and torture, Jesus experienced no pain on the cross. Rather, he was in ecstasy. He knew that he was not his body. As for the witnesses, however, they could only project their own fear upon what they saw. The story was written down and passed on. Had there been no crucifixion, nobody would know of Jesus today. Adding to the drama, his body disappears. Now, you have an unjustifiable execution, but there were many of those with the Romans. How to make this one stand out? Let's disappear the body, right under the nose of the Roman sentries. Then to cap things off, let's have the body reappear later. This is the stuff that sells newspapers, not to speak of Bibles. Jesus simply, out of love and trust, followed the plan that came from Spirit. He did this, not to pay for your sins, but to teach you how to listen to Spirit, how to trust, and as an act of faith. Some of you have the terror that if you listen to Spirit you'll end up nailed to a cross, too. You may have something to move through around this. It is the ego that leads you to pain and suffering, not Spirit.

How would your life change if you trusted in the true story of Jesus? When you think of Easter, the message is of love and eternal life. The focus is on the resurrection. If your thoughts go to crucifixion and suffering, ask Spirit to lift those thoughts from you. It is time on a symbolic level to burn all of your crosses. As long as you hold onto the cross as the symbol of Christianity and Jesus, your life will be one of sacrifice and suffering. Burn the cross. Burn them all. Let that blaze be the fire of the love of the eternal flame of God.

God Blesses You,

Sanhia

What is the difference between ascension and enlightenment?

I have been talking about ascension for a long time. This has been the major focus since I began communicating through Michael over thirty years ago. For those of you whose native language is Swedish, there is no word that directly translates this concept. The closest is "himlafärd", which means "a trip to heaven". This provides a beginning in grasping the term, but still contains a sense of going somewhere. In English, ascending literally means to go up, again indicating the involvement of motion. A clearer understanding would be to associate ascension with the realization of your divine nature. The idea of "going up" assumes that your ascension is not right here, right now. The thought of having to travel to find your ascension only leaves you separate from its realization. However, there is also an accuracy in these literal translations because when you fully realize your divine nature, this earth plane loses any reality it might have previously held for you. In the challenging attempt to define ascension, I have often talked about what it isn't. Ascension is not something that is realized through following specific practices, disciplines, or beliefs. It does not happen because you are good, or because you do things in the right way. Ascension is the full realization that you are one with God, you are loved unconditionally, you *are* love, that there *is* only love.

I have talked about all of this before, but today I wish to introduce another term which is commonly used and, at times, seems to be interchangeable with ascension. That word is enlightenment, which in Swedish translates as "upplysning", meaning "putting the spotlight on", a more direct translation. I want to compare these terms, beginning with a disclaimer. The differentiation I will establish is connected to the manner in which I define these words. Other sources may have different definitions. Enlightenment could be seen as a subset of ascension. All who realize their ascension are also, certainly, enlightened. However, those who are enlightened do not necessarily realize their ascension. What is the difference? Enlightenment means that you realize that this physical plane is all illusion. You understand that you are the creator of all that you experience. You know that time doesn't truly exist, nor does your physical body. You realize that you *are*. That is your only truth. You always *are*. That full awareness is called enlightenment. Often, enlightenment is seen as the highest spiritual goal. It is a term that is used within the Buddhist tradition. The Buddha became enlightened, and so Buddhists seek a similar experience.

If you experience enlightenment, you continue to deal with the world about you, but with an absolutely different perspective. You are still in a body dealing with everyday life, but you no longer take it seriously. The only thing that remains real is self. You know that you always *are*. The enlightened one has no idea whether others have any true existence. I wouldn't know if there is such a thing as "you", an entity that also creates everything that you see. All that I can know is that your existence is my creation. In ascension, you have this enlightened perspective, but here is a distinction. When we speak of enlightenment, there is usually no reference to God. There is only the "light", the eternal is-ness. The assumption of the enlightened one may be that the existence of God is beyond knowing, that all that can be known for sure is the existence of self. There are no answers to any of the deep questions such as: "Why do I exist?" "Where did I come from?" or "Why did I create this body and this universe?" Some who are enlightened will argue that your existence is all you can know. This knowingness of the unreality of the human experience allows almost all pain to evaporate.

The difference with ascension is that it does deal with these questions. It recognizes divinity and a creative source, which I call God. It understands that the earth experience and physical creations emanate not from God, but from the souls we call human. This manifestation came out of fear of God and separation from Him. We created this universe to hide from God, out of our fear of punishment. Without the acceptance of the existence of God, you can realize that all of this is a movie, but still have a vague sense of emptiness. The deep questions do not totally disappear. Strands of judgment persist. In fact, enlightenment might be the last refuge of the ego. The answer to the deep questions is that you are here to heal your relationship with your Creator. Denial of His existence won't make Him go away. He has nowhere to go. Nor do you. This understanding allows you to ask God, or Spirit, for support in aligning with truth, in reconnecting to your divinity. You realize the importance of forgiveness in the process. You become absolutely intolerant of the slightest judgments you might hold. You seek to see divinity everywhere.

There has been a great confusion because most of those who believe in God do not believe in enlightenment, while most of those who believe in enlightenment don't believe in God. Ascension requires both beliefs. The connective energy is unconditional love. Without God, unconditional love may not be of importance. You could be enlightened, but not fully surrendered to and guided by Spirit. The void or emptiness of the enlightened state allows a place for the voice of ego, because your mind has not been fully offered to Spirit. In Buddhism, there exist bodhisattvas who are on the threshold of enlightenment but hold back, waiting for everyone to join them. They reincarnate over and over, coming as teachers. The confusion is that one's primary reason for incarnating becomes the serving of others. This is in denial of God and your separation. It is the lack of recognition that what you see in others is only a reflection of yourself, which is all that you can affect. The ascended masters comprehended that their own realization of divinity was the reason for their physical experience. Ironically, their ascension is also the greatest gift they could offer to others in supporting spiritual development. Ascension understands the oneness. It knows that personal ascension raises all ships, shines light on all souls.

God Blesses You,

Sanhia

What tools are there for realizing ascension?

You deserve to be in a place of joy, love, and peace. The ego always pulls you away from your true inheritance from God. What is certain is that you will ascend; you will realize your divinity. You will know true joy, love, and peace. People have asked how they can shorten the period in the meantime in which they are suffering and in fear.

I am presenting you with a short list of things that you may do to help speed up the chasing away of the ego and the welcoming of your divine self. I present this not in the spirit of burdening you with more thoughts about what you should be doing, but to offer you some inspirational choices. As you move toward realizing your ascension, your moments of pain will be spread further apart and will be of shorter duration. Your go-to place will be joyful, loving and accepting of whatever is present.

First are some suggestions for how to deal with all the lists in your life. I expect that most of you have lists, whether written or mental. Some of the experts suggest that the way to handle your lists is to tackle the toughest thing first. The thinking is that when the biggest challenge is out of the way, everything else becomes easier. Of course, the next thing you take on is what is now the biggest challenge. I think this orientation is backwards. Look at your list and ask yourself what would be the most fun thing to do. What would give you the most joy and excitement? Or ask what is the easiest thing for you to do? You do that task first. After experiencing the joy of crossing something off your list, check to see what is now the most fun and easy thing. That is all you do. Of course, your list will never be finished: you will always be adding more things to it, but the choosing remains the same. It is not a question of what has been on your list longest or what most "needs" to be done. The choice is always determined by your passion. If you believe that life is a struggle, choosing the hard things first will re-affirm that creed. You think that if you just force yourself to do these tasks you have been putting off, your life will ease up and you can enjoy things. The truth is that your list will keep growing, as will your certainty that this is just how life is. If the habit you nurture is to look at your list and ask what would be fun to do today, what is most exciting – your whole attitude toward life will begin to shift. You deserve to do what you came here to do, and that "doing" will be a joyful experience.

I recommend that you treat the list I am about to give in that manner. There are more things on it than you could do every day. "Cherry pick" the ones that most appeal to you and play with them first. There is no order of importance to the items.

1. **Intention**: Have you made your intention to realize your divinity? If not, the pain will not begin to end until you commit to joy and ascension. If so, there is no need to repeat the request. However, as you are looking at whatever is troubling you or whatever logs you have thrown in front of yourself for the day, ask yourself how all this connects with your intention. That is the important question. The task is to align yourself with what you want. Perhaps this means letting go of something. Maybe you are giving importance to matters that are not connected to the truth of who you are. Are you are being true to yourself? Give everything to Spirit.

2. **The *five-step process*** (see p. 230): If you are not feeling good, emotionally or physically, do the process. Go through it on your own, or listen to the recording on www.channelswithoutborders.com/5-step-process/, or contact one of your friends to lead you through it. Decide that you don't wish to live with the discomfort; change your story. Remember that the fear that you transform to love through *Spiritual Alchemy* is permanently altered. You have accumulated a finite amount of fear in your body. It is only a matter of time before love rules your day instead of fear.

3. **Numerology chart - Your Love Letter from your Higher Self:** There are many different ways that you can play with your chart. You could pick any major position in your chart and ask for guidance concerning a situation you are dealing with. Or you could pick one position at a time and think and meditate on it. Eventually you might work through your entire chart. Focusing on the name numbers will help you accept, support, and love yourself, while looking at the birth numbers can assist you in accepting what you have created or drawn into your life. Allow Spirit to talk with you through the numbers. Your *Ascension Numerology* book will assist you as you begin this process, but eventually the numbers and positions will become such a part of you that you will only refer to the book occasionally.

4. **Spiritually inspiring reading:** Find an inspirational book to read out of daily, perhaps in the morning as a way to start off your day. You may have a particular favorite or might move from one book to another. Ask your friends for recommendations. You can read from this book. Reading regularly helps align your brain-mind with Spirit instead of the ego.

5. *A Course in Miracles:* I have separated this out from inspirational reading, because the *Course* is a particular study. It is designed to be worked with in small blocks of time on a daily basis. I see the *Course* as a spiritual equivalent to a workout at the gym, A day here and there will not make much difference. But years of regular training will perform *Miracles* with your body or with your spiritual awareness. We could call it spiritual toning. It takes quite a while to turn around the ship of mass consciousness. If you stay with the *Course*, the ego doesn't have a prayer.

6. **Forgiveness**: Practice forgiveness daily, constantly. Separation evaporates. Forgive yourself; forgive others. Forgive God; forgive the weather. Forgive the driver for hanging out in the left-hand lane. Forgive everyone, everything all of the time. You do this not because the forgiveness is needed, because everyone, including yourself, is innocent, but because when you forgive, it allows a place to align with Spirit. When you are judging yourself or others you are separate from Spirit. That places you in hell. When you are in hell you are suffering. The ego will tell you "that bastard deserves it"; he deserves your anger and your judgment. The ego loves righteous indignation. It creates enemies and separation. Forgiveness is the quickest way. Everything in your life that is painful is connected to a lack of forgiveness. Every physical ailment you have is linked to not being able to forgive. If you are having trouble forgiving, ask Spirit for help. In the end, as well as in the beginning, there is nothing to forgive. There is only innocence.

7. **See the perfection**: See the perfection in each person and each situation you meet. They are here to support your ascension. The driver who just cut you off was the perfect driver for you at this moment. You have the perfect President. Everything is perfect. That plane crashing with no survivors was a perfect event. Divine, as it should be. The *dis-ease*, whatever it is…perfect. Accepting perfection is the greatest threat to the ego. The ego's job is to protect you from imperfections. It uses your judgment and your anger to accomplish this. Perfection puts the ego out of work. With the recognition of perfection, you can no longer be a victim to anything. Negative patterns will disappear from your life. There is nothing left to fear. This is heavenly. It doesn't matter whether

you understand why something is perfect, that knowing will come in time. Just trust. Nothing has to change.

8. **Accept God**: This doesn't make any difference to God, but it makes an enormous difference for you. Here is how I know that people fear God, even if they claim to be atheists. If they hold a speck of judgment, they believe in and fear God, a punishing God. People consciously deny the existence of God because they have made Him in their image. They think that God is judgmental and vengeful. They blame God for what humans have created...which is everything that exists in the physical world. They deny God because judgmental people claim to speak for God. Separate all of these ego lies about God from the truth, which is so simple. God is unconditional love. There is nothing that God would ever judge. Claim God. Reunite with Him.

If you pick just one of the items on this list, the one that most draws you, it will make an enormous difference in your life. When you are ready to take on more, you will know. If you skip a day, forgive yourself and start over. God doesn't care.

God Blesses You,

Sanhia

Biography

Michael Hersey has been working personally with his own ascension process since the early '70s. He was guided to study numerology and to establish a practice in 1979. Michael also developed a workshop program which supported others to give up their fears about money and do the work they came here to do. He began channeling ascended master Sanhia in 1985, and has channeled for numerous groups and individuals throughout the United States and Sweden. Since 2013 he has co-led *Spiritual Alchemy* groups with his partner Ulla Lindgren. The focus of all the work is on realizing your personal divinity. Michael is also the author of the book *Ascension Numerology: A Love Letter from your Higher Self.*

Ascension Numerology

Ascension Numerology brings ancient wisdom into the 21st century by presenting a strong focus on your spiritual intention, particularly through the Ascension Number. It introduces key concepts such as the *"Love Letter from Your Higher Self"*, and the message that you are the creator of your life. You have been planning this adventure for a long time. During the pre-planning you set things up to encourage the likelihood of you realizing your ascension. This information is available to you through your numerology chart. New insights await long-time students of numerology, while new students will find simplicity and clarity guiding them into an intuitive grasp of their charts. And all readers are empowered to go deeper on their own with this cutting edge book. A new dimension is the use of multiple color graphic representations to speak directly to your right brain. This book is fun!

You can find out more about *Ascension Numerology* at: www.channelswithoutborders.com/ascension-numerology-book/ or order it from your favorite online bookstore.

ACKNOWLEDGEMENTS

This book would not have been possible in its present form without the contributions of Ulla Lindgren. I considered listing her as co-author, but she said that the original text all comes from Sanhia or from me. Nevertheless, not one word made it into print without Ulla's consideration. For one whom English is a second tongue – and who claims to not be very proficient at it – she has an amazing feel and command of the language and its nuances. Ulla's contributions included word choice, sentence structure, ruthless slashing of unnecessary text, and – above all – consistency to Sanhia's ascension message. She also was at least an equal partner in choices for the cover, layout, and font. Her willingness to follow my relentless schedule of editing and reediting messages allowed the book to be born this year.

When Sanhia announced that a collection of his messages would be the next book, I initially thought that it would be a walk in the park after our labors on Ascension Numerology. A mini-marathon ended up being a better description. I did learn a lot more about how the co-creation process works with Sanhia. It would be so nice if he just dictated in word perfect form as many others do through their channels. But no, Sanhia wants me to be more involved with the process, as a part of my training. After recording an interview with Sanhia, which takes twenty to thirty minutes, I spend a half day transcribing that into the format that becomes the monthly message. Ulla and I go over it together. Sometimes that goes quite smoothly. Other times it becomes quite a vehicle for working out the spiritual issues in our relationship. Sanhia is always there to give us a loving push into our process. I can say that the final result that comes out of all of that matches the growth that we each experience alone and as a couple.

Working, perhaps playing is a more accurate term, with Marie Örnesved is always a joy for us. Our work sessions usually began with an hour of informal sharing and mutual support. Sometimes Sanhia is invited in. Marie is above all in her pro-fessionalism and efficiency, but at the same time is open to whatever intuitive guidance she receives as we create the book. Not only does she freely offer whatever insights come to her, and defends them vigorously – she also lovingly defers to us to make the final call. Marie will spare no effort to make every nuance of the book live up to the highest standard. She had a hand in many of the stylistic decisions we made including having themes and underscored index terms, re-titling the messages in a more informative question format, as well as the cover art, font and the numbering style. We feel gifted to be working with Marie and LightSpira.

Stella Hansen has again offered incredible support as our editor. Stella offered years ago to donate her services in editing the monthly messages, as her eagle eye always noticed small (and some not so small) errors. Stella went through all of these messages two more times. She not only catches the repeated word, the missed comma, and misused punctuation, but she also contributes meaningful questions about the content and lets me know when a concept has not been clearly explained. Her years of work with Sanhia are of great value to us (and to her, I think).

I also wish to thank Mary Grace for her suggestion that led to the beginning of the monthly messages. Barb Daugherty provided a great assistance in helping me set up the format and the mailing list through Mail Chimp. Patricia Hersey contributed her time by taking dictation for the earlier messages. Thanks to different readers who have offered suggestions for topics. The *Spiritual Alchemy* groups have generated wonderful subjects for messages in the past few years through their questions to Sanhia and his responses.

Finally I want to give thanks to Spirit for guidance, to *A Course in Miracles* for daily inspiration, and, of course, to Sanhia. He wants me to say that his job is the easiest of all, talking for twenty to thirty minutes once a month about the subject that holds the greatest passion for him – ascension. He says that he left all the heavy lifting to me, and to Ulla. I am grateful for the workout.

The five-step process

1 Define the area in your life that is causing you emotional, spiritual, mental, and/or physical pain. This will be referred to as your "old story". State it succinctly in, preferably, a single sentence. Saying it out loud is good. Your "old story" is what your brain-mind thinks is true. Sometimes you are carrying uncomfortable energy in your body, but don't know what "old story" it is connected to. In such cases your "old story" is that you have this pain in your body. Then go on to the second step.

2 Focus on where you feel the discomfort in your body when you think of your "old story". Close your eyes, relax, breathe slowly and deeply, and turn off your brain-mind. You can do this by imagining you have a switch on the side of your head. See yourself flipping it to the off position. Now, watch the discomfort from your belly-mind. Do not judge, label, or try to to get rid of the feeling. Simply accept it, let it be, and let it do whatever it wishes to do. Become one with the sensation and embrace it with love. Stay with the energy until you notice the nature of it changing. When the feeling becomes calm, perhaps warmer and lighter; move the energy to your heart chakra. Then, on your exhales, see it move slowly out of your heart chakra through a laser-like beam out into the universe. Continue breathing until the energy is largely dissipated.

3 Take full responsibility for having created your "old story", knowing that as you are a divine being it could be no other way. Taking responsibility out loud is good. Even though you may not yet understand why, remind yourself that the creation came out of love, choosing the best way for you to realize your divinity.

4 From the depth of your heart hear your new story. State it positively and in the present tense. Don't require any individual to play a certain role in your story. If you want another to be involved, describe the role without naming the actor. Trust Spirit to find the one who will fit. Your job is to express your story. Spirit's job is to bring it into your life. State this new story succinctly in, preferably, a single sentence. Saying it out loud is good. It should fill you with feelings of love, peace, and joy. If it doesn't, find a way to restate until it does.

5 You aren't always able to get to the deepest level of your story at once. Therefore, your "old story" could come back at some point in the future. If so, congratulate yourself for noticing it and as soon as possible begin the five-step process over again. Know that the energy that has been transformed from fear into love is permanent, while your pain is finite. Eventually there will be no reason for repetition.

You can listen to a recording which leads you through the *five-step process* on our website:

www.channelswithoutborders.com/5-step-process/

Themes

Messages are not organized in any particular fashion and each one might deal with a variety of different themes, while answering a specific question. On these pages are all of the themes, each with a chronological listing of related messages for your deeper exploration. Major themes are indicated by a dark gray field, while the minor themes list which major theme they are associated with. I can't stress enough that repeated reading, accompanied by reflection and meditation will assist you in integrating these concepts into your being.

Acceptance (subtheme of Judgment)
Letting go of resistance to what is

1. What is true thankfulness?
6. What is the most appropriate way to honor Jesus?
8. Why is forgiveness important?
17. What does attachment mean?
27. Is there really going to be a Last Judgment?
30. Is it possible to ascend and be in a relationship?
39. How can I feel more grateful?
42. What can I do about my *dis-ease* or ailment?
44. How do I create *dis-ease*?
47. How can I realize my purpose?
51. Why is intention necessary?
57. Is there divinity in everyone?
58. What can I do when things are less than perfect?
60. Do you believe in a punishing God?
69. What do birthdays and deathdays have in common?
81. What tools are there for realizing ascension?

Ascension
The reason you are here; realizing your divinity, your oneness with God

5. Can I follow my passions?
6. What is the most appropriate way to honor Jesus?
9. What is confused in Christianity?
11. Can I love myself into ascension?
22. What is the first step toward realizing my ascension?
23. Why do I have so much drama in my life?
25. What about the planetary ascension of 2012?
26. Have you chosen ascension?
29. Do I deserve to have what I want?
30. Is it possible to ascend and be in a relationship?
36. How do my relationships fit into my ascension path?
40. Are you afraid of the dark?
44. How do I create *dis-ease*?
48. Are aging and death certain?
49. How important are special places and secret teachings?
54. What do you mean when you say I pre-planned this life?
55. What can help me to forgive?
61. What is a spiritual response to a world crisis?
67. How do my home and relationships affect my intention to ascend?
70. How can I deal with my karma?
71. Why doesn't money feel spiritual to me?
72. Who are you?
75. What is the difference between unity and oneness?
76. Why do I feel abandoned by God?
77. How do I discern Spirit from ego?
80. What is the difference between ascension and enlightenment?
81. What tools are there for realizing ascension?

Attachment (subtheme of Physical Body)
The false belief that you need something or someone in order to be happy

17. What does attachment mean?
23. Why do I have so much drama in my life?
25. What about the planetary ascension of 2012?
26. Have you chosen ascension?
36. How do my relationships fit into my ascension path?

Christianity (subtheme of Separation)

Religion that fails to comprehend the true teachings of Jesus, instead preaching there is separation between you and God

6. What is the most appropriate way to honor Jesus?
9. What is confused in Christianity?
20. Can you suggest a prayer for ascension?
27. Is there really going to be a Last Judgment?
62. How do I deal with the religious conflict in the Middle East?

63. How should I celebrate Christmas?
70. How can I deal with my karma?
76. Why do I feel abandoned by God?
78. Does love require me to sacrifice?
79. Did Jesus die for our sins?

Commitment (subtheme of Creation)

Staying with an intention until you achieve it or choose a new intention

13. How can I get more joy in my life?
30. Is it possible to ascend and be in a relationship?
51. Why is intention necessary?

65. Why is it hard to let go of victimhood?
81. What tools are there for realizing ascension?

Creation

Everything in your world is your manifestation

4. Are there ghosts or evil spirits?
8. Why is forgiveness important?
9. What is confused in Christianity?
10. Is there a conflict between politics and spirituality?
12. Will I ever fully heal myself?
14. What can I do when I feel like a victim?
16. How can I protect omyself from natural disasters?

18. How can numerology support me on my ascension path?
24. How do I deal with power out of balance?
27. Is there really going to be a Last Judgment?
36. How do my relationships fit into my ascension path?
37. What can I gain by letting go of control?
38. Is suffering a necessary part of my spiritual path?

Deservedness (subtheme of Divine Nature)
God offers you everything without any effort on your part

Divine Nature
You are the image of God, a being of unconditional love and unlimited creativity

Ego (subtheme of Fear)

A terrified voice you listen to that thinks you are separate from God, and doesn't believe in your divinity

Fear

An insane response to a non-existent threat, the cause of all suffering

Five-Step Process (subtheme of Fear)
Developed by Sanhia to transform fear into love, falseness into truth

43. How can I get the ying and yang energy in harmony within me?
44. How do I create *dis-ease*?
45. How do I deal with my environmental fears?
47. How can I realize my purpose?
48. Are aging and death certain?
50. How can I step out of the mass consciousness?
51. Why is intention necessary?
53. How do violence and guilt relate to sexuality?
54. What do you mean when you say I pre-planned this life?
56. Why is it important to balance my masculine and feminine energy?
58. What can I do when things are less than perfect?
59. How can I reduce stress in my life?
60. Do you believe in a punishing God?
64. What do you mean by my "old story"?
66. How does the ego divide and conquer?

Forgiveness (subtheme of Ascension)

Releasing blame directed at yourself or others, the realization that all are innocent and that no harm was done

8. Why is forgiveness important?
21. Why should I take responsibility for what others do to me?
55. What can help me to forgive?
60. Do you believe in a punishing God?
68. Can you explain the terms ego and Spirit?
70. How can I deal with my karma?
74. What can I do with the fear I feel over Trump's election?
75. What is the difference between unity and oneness?
81. What tools are there for realizing ascension?

Gift (subtheme of Love)

Realizing that everything that comes into your life is a present for you to assist in realizing your divine nature

17. What does attachment mean?
21. Why should I take responsibility for what others do to me?
22. What is the first step toward realizing my ascension?
30. Is it possible to ascend and be in a relationship?
32. Where is my true home?
34. What am I do with death?
37. What can I gain by letting go of control?

39. How can I feel more grateful?
42. What can I do about my *dis-ease* or ailment?
54. What do you mean when you say I pre-planned this life?
61. What is a spiritual response to a world crisis?
69. What do birthdays and deathdays have in common?
70. How can I deal with my karma?
73. How do I move from a lack of faith to trust?

Gratitude (subtheme of Love)

Feeling thankful for everything that happens to you, gratefulness for everything God has given you

1. What is true thankfulness?
37. What can I gain by letting go of control?
39. How can I feel more grateful?
42. What can I do about my *dis-ease* or ailment?
69. What do birthdays and deathdays have in common?
73. How do I move from a lack of faith to trust?

Guilt (subtheme of Judgment)

The belief and strong accompanying feelings that you have done something wrong and will be punished

8. Why is forgiveness important?
53. How do violence and guilt relate to sexuality?
60. Do you believe in a punishing God?
61. What is a spiritual response to a world crisis?
65. Why is it hard to let go of victimhood?
68. Can you explain the terms ego and Spirit?
70. How can I deal with my karma?
78. Does love require me to sacrifice?

Health (subtheme of Physical Body)

All dis-ease is of your creation, good health is your birthright

16. How can I protect omyself from natural disasters?
35. Why do negative things keep happening to me?
40. Are you afraid of the dark?
42. What can I do about my *dis-ease* or ailment?
44. How do I create *dis-ease*?
48. Are aging and death certain?

Home (subtheme of Physical Body)
It nurtures you if it truly is

30. Is it possible to ascend and be in a relationship?
32. Where is my true home?

67. How do my home and relationships affect my intention to ascend?

Illusion (subtheme of Separation)
Your perception of things that don't exist, such as the world, fear, and death

2. What is the most valuable gift to give?
3. Will the earth survive?
4. Are there ghosts or evil spirits?
9. What is confused in Christianity?
23. Why do I have so much drama in my life?
25. What about the planetary ascension of 2012?
26. Have you chosen ascension?
27. Is there really going to be a Last Judgment?
34. What am I do with death?
48. Are aging and death certain?

55. What can help me to forgive?
60. Do you believe in a punishing God?
68. Can you explain the terms ego and Spirit?
69. What do birthdays and deathdays have in common?
71. Why doesn't money feel spiritual to me?
75. What is the difference between unity and oneness?
76. Why do I feel abandoned by God?

Innocence (subtheme of Divine Nature)
Your true and constant state, the way in which God sees you

8. Why is forgiveness important?
32. Where is my true home?
63. How should I celebrate Christmas?

64. What do you mean by my "old story"?
72. Who are you?
81. What tools are there for realizing ascension?

Intention (subtheme of Creation)
What you decide what you will do, communicating to Spirit what you wish to manifest

5. Can I follow my passions?
19. Why have religions been male dominated?
22. What is the first step toward realizing my ascension?
23. Why do I have so much drama in my life?
30. Is it possible to ascend and be in a relationship?
44. How do I create *dis-ease*?
51. Why is intention necessary?
58. What can I do when things are less than perfect?

67. How do my home and relationships affect my intention to ascend?
68. Can you explain the terms ego and Spirit?
73. How do I move from a lack of faith to trust?
77. How do I discern Spirit from ego?
81. What tools are there for realizing ascension?

Jesus (subtheme of Divine Nature)
Ascended master, author of "A Course in Miracles", teacher of Sanhia, best known teacher of ascension

2. What is the most valuable gift to give?
6. What is the most appropriate way to honor Jesus?
9. What is confused in Christianity?
10. Is there a conflict between politics and spirituality?
19. Why have religions been male dominated?
25. What about the planetary ascension of 2012?
31. How can I change the world?
38. Is suffering a necessary part of my spiritual path?
46. What are the real dynamics of rescuing?
49. How important are special places and secret teachings?
50. How can I step out of the mass consciousness?

51. Why is intention necessary?
52. Do I have to choose between spirituality and sexuality?
55. What can help me to forgive?
62. How do I deal with the religious conflict in the Middle East?
63. How should I celebrate Christmas?
76. Why do I feel abandoned by God?
77. How do I discern Spirit from ego?
78. Does love require me to sacrifice?
79. Did Jesus die for our sins?

Judgment

Believing there is such a thing as right and wrong, deciding what and who fits in either category

Love

Truth, the natural state, God, all you need

out of balance?

Masculine and Feminine (subtheme of Physical Body)
The two poles in the physical world, find the balance

Mass Consciousness (subtheme of Story)
Societal beliefs that run your life

43. How can I get the ying and yang energy in harmony within me?
47. How can I realize my purpose?
48. Are aging and death certain?
50. How can I step out of the mass consciousness?
53. How do violence and guilt relate to sexuality?
55. What can help me to forgive?
56. Why is it important to balance my masculine and feminine energy?
60. Do you believe in a punishing God?
67. How do my home and relationships affect my intention to ascend?
72. Who are you?
77. How do I discern Spirit from ego?
78. Does love require me to sacrifice?
81. What tools are there for realizing ascension?

Mirror (subtheme of Judgment)
Wherever you look, there you are

16. How can I protect omyself from natural disasters?
30. Is it possible to ascend and be in a relationship?
31. How can I change the world?
51. Why is intention necessary?
55. What can help me to forgive?
57. Is there divinity in everyone?
62. How do I deal with the religious conflict in the Middle East?
67. How do my home and relationships affect my intention to ascend?
68. Can you explain the terms ego and Spirit?

Movie (subtheme of Story)
Life is just a picture show, it's your movie

23. Why do I have so much drama in my life?
26. Have you chosen ascension?
27. Is there really going to be a Last Judgment?
30. Is it possible to ascend and be in a relationship?
62. How do I deal with the religious conflict in the Middle East?
71. Why doesn't money feel spiritual to me?
80. What is the difference between ascension and enlightenment?

Oneness (subtheme of Divine Nature)
Another definition of truth, all is one, you are one with God

4. Are there ghosts or evil spirits?
68. Can you explain the terms ego and Spirit?
75. What is the difference between unity and oneness?
76. Why do I feel abandoned by God?
80. What is the difference between ascension and enlightenment?

Passion (subtheme of Love)
Your inner drive, one way Spirit speaks to you

5. Can I follow my passions?
7. Do I deserve to have my desires fulfilled?
12. Will I ever fully heal myself?
13. How can I get more joy in my life?
17. What does attachment mean?
20. Can you suggest a prayer for ascension?
28. What is meant by Right Livelihood?
29. Do I deserve to have what I want?
35. Why do negative things keep happening to me?
59. How can I reduce stress in my life?
81. What tools are there for realizing ascension?

Perfection (subtheme of Ascension)
The natural state of the world, the truth about everything that happens

1. What is true thankfulness?
12. Will I ever fully heal myself?
14. What can I do when I feel like a victim?
16. How can I protect omyself from natural disasters?
17. What does attachment mean?
20. Can you suggest a prayer for ascension?
57. Is there divinity in everyone?
58. What can I do when things are less than perfect?
62. How do I deal with the religious conflict in the Middle East?
73. How do I move from a lack of faith to trust?
74. What can I do with the fear I feel over Trump's election?
76. Why do I feel abandoned by God?
81. What tools are there for realizing ascension?

Physical Body

You are not your body

4. Are there ghosts or evil spirits?
9. What is confused in Christianity?
12. Will I ever fully heal myself?
21. Why should I take responsibility for what others do to me?
23. Why do I have so much drama in my life?
33. Is it helpful to honor the feminine energy?
34. What am I do with death?
36. How do my relationships fit into my ascension path?
40. Are you afraid of the dark?
41. How does manifestation take place?
42. What can I do about my *dis-ease* or ailment?
43. How can I get the ying and yang energy in harmony within me?
44. How do I create *dis-ease*?
45. How do I deal with my environmental fears?
48. Are aging and death certain?
51. Why is intention necessary?
54. What do you mean when you say I pre-planned this life?
60. Do you believe in a punishing God?
64. What do you mean by my "old story"?
69. What do birthdays and deathdays have in common?
71. Why doesn't money feel spiritual to me?
72. Who are you?
74. What can I do with the fear I feel over Trump's election?
76. Why do I feel abandoned by God?
79. Did Jesus die for our sins?

Power (subtheme of Creation)

The intersection of love and intention

10. Is there a conflict between politics and spirituality?
15. What was the Arab Spring about?
21. Why should I take responsibility for what others do to me?
24. How do I deal with power out of balance?
31. How can I change the world?
33. Is it helpful to honor the feminine energy?
37. What can I gain by letting go of control?

Pre-planning (subtheme of Ascension)

You set up this lifetime

Purpose (subtheme of Ascension)

What you are here to do

Reality (subtheme of Separation)

Your nature is divine, nothing in the world is real

1. What is true thankfulness?
4. Are there ghosts or evil spirits?
10. Is there a conflict between politics and spirituality?
18. How can numerology support me on my ascension path?
24. How do I deal with power out of balance?
27. Is there really going to be a Last Judgment?
35. Why do negative things keep happening to me?
43. How can I get the ying and yang energy in harmony within me?
55. What can help me to forgive?
59. How can I reduce stress in my life?
60. Do you believe in a punishing God?
61. What is a spiritual response to a world crisis?
76. Why do I feel abandoned by God?
80. What is the difference between ascension and enlightenment?

Relationships (subtheme of Story)

They are intended to support your spiritual growth

7. Do I deserve to have my desires fulfilled?
22. What is the first step toward realizing my ascension?
25. What about the planetary ascension of 2012?
30. Is it possible to ascend and be in a relationship?
36. How do my relationships fit into my ascension path?
40. Are you afraid of the dark?
53. How do violence and guilt relate to sexuality?
54. What do you mean when you say I pre-planned this life?
65. Why is it hard to let go of victimhood?
67. How do my home and relationships affect my intention to ascend?
71. Why doesn't money feel spiritual to me?
78. Does love require me to sacrifice?

Responsibility (subtheme of Creation)

Not just a good idea, it is the law

19. Why have religions been male dominated?
21. Why should I take responsibility for what others do to me?
30. Is it possible to ascend and be in a relationship?
31. How can I change the world?
32. Where is my true home?
34. What am I do with death?
35. Why do negative things keep happening to me?
38. Is suffering a necessary part of my spiritual path?
41. How does manifestation take place?

42. What can I do about my *dis-ease* or ailment?
43. How can I get the ying and yang energy in harmony within me?
54. What do you mean when you say I pre-planned this life?
57. Is there divinity in everyone?
59. How can I reduce stress in my life?
61. What is a spiritual response to a world crisis?
65. Why is it hard to let go of victimhood?

Right and Wrong (subtheme of Judgment)

Belief in this is the original sin

52. Do I have to choose between spirituality and sexuality?
60. Do you believe in a punishing God?

70. How can I deal with my karma?
75. What is the difference between unity and oneness?

Right Livelihood (subtheme of Love)

The loving service you came here to do

7. Do I deserve to have my desires fulfilled?
28. What is meant by Right Livelihood?
29. Do I deserve to have what I want?

47. How can I realize my purpose?
71. Why doesn't money feel spiritual to me?

Separation

False belief that keeps you stuck in hell

4. Are there ghosts or evil spirits?
8. Why is forgiveness important?
9. What is confused in Christianity?
20. Can you suggest a prayer for ascension?
39. How can I feel more grateful?
43. How can I get the ying and yang energy in harmony within me?
49. How important are special places and secret teachings?
53. How do violence and guilt relate to sexuality?
55. What can help me to forgive?
59. How can I reduce stress in my life?
60. Do you believe in a punishing God?
65. Why is it hard to let go of victimhood?
68. Can you explain the terms ego and Spirit?
71. Why doesn't money feel spiritual to me?
73. How do I move from a lack of faith to trust?
75. What is the difference between unity and oneness?
76. Why do I feel abandoned by God?
78. Does love require me to sacrifice?
79. Did Jesus die for our sins?
80. What is the difference between ascension and enlightenment?
81. What tools are there for realizing ascension?

Spiritual Alchemy (subtheme of Fear)

Process of transmuting fear into love

38. Is suffering a necessary part of my spiritual path?
39. How can I feel more grateful?
41. How does manifestation take place?
43. How can I get the ying and yang energy in harmony within me?
44. How do I create *dis-ease*?
45. How do I deal with my environmental fears?
51. Why is intention necessary?
54. What do you mean when you say I pre-planned this life?
64. What do you mean by my "old story"?
81. What tools are there for realizing ascension?

Story

Personal belief that creates your "reality"

9. What is confused in Christianity?
23. Why do I have so much drama in my life?
35. Why do negative things keep happening to me?
36. How do my relationships fit into my ascension path?
39. How can I feel more grateful?
41. How does manifestation take place?
42. What can I do about my *disease* or ailment?
43. How can I get the ying and yang energy in harmony within me?
46. What are the real dynamics of rescuing?
47. How can I realize my purpose?
48. Are aging and death certain?
50. How can I step out of the mass consciousness?
52. Do I have to choose between spirituality and sexuality?
54. What do you mean when you say I pre-planned this life?
56. Why is it important to balance my masculine and feminine energy?
58. What can I do when things are less than perfect?
59. How can I reduce stress in my life?
64. What do you mean by my "old story"?
65. Why is it hard to let go of victimhood?
66. How does the ego divide and conquer?
71. Why doesn't money feel spiritual to me?
72. Who are you?
79. Did Jesus die for our sins?

Trust and Faith (subtheme of Separation)

The bridge between the human and the divine

1. What is true thankfulness?
2. What is the most valuable gift to give?
3. Will the earth survive?
5. Can I follow my passions?
14. What can I do when I feel like a victim?
15. What was the Arab Spring about?
17. What does attachment mean?
20. Can you suggest a prayer for ascension?
22. What is the first step toward realizing my ascension?

28. What is meant by Right Livelihood?
37. What can I gain by letting go of control?
46. What are the real dynamics of rescuing?
68. Can you explain the terms ego and Spirit?
71. Why doesn't money feel spiritual to me?

73. How do I move from a lack of faith to trust?
74. What can I do with the fear I feel over Trump's election?
77. How do I discern Spirit from ego?
79. Did Jesus die for our sins?

Victimhood (subtheme of Story)

The illusion that things can happen to you without your permission

4. Are there ghosts or evil spirits?
8. Why is forgiveness important?
10. Is there a conflict between politics and spirituality?
14. What can I do when I feel like a victim?
16. How can I protect omyself from natural disasters?
17. What does attachment mean?
21. Why should I take responsibility for what others do to me?
34. What am I do with death?
39. How can I feel more grateful?
42. What can I do about my *disease* or ailment?

43. How can I get the ying and yang energy in harmony within me?
45. How do I deal with my environmental fears?
46. What are the real dynamics of rescuing?
51. Why is intention necessary?
53. How do violence and guilt relate to sexuality?
54. What do you mean when you say I pre-planned this life?
61. What is a spiritual response to a world crisis?
62. How do I deal with the religious conflict in the Middle East?
65. Why is it hard to let go of victimhood?

World Events (subtheme of Fear)

A spiritual perspective on major world happenings

3. Will the earth survive?
10. Is there a conflict between politics and spirituality?
15. What was the Arab Spring about?
16. How can I protect omyself from natural disasters?
19. Why have religions been male dominated?
25. What about the planetary ascension of 2012?
31. How can I change the world?
33. Is it helpful to honor the feminine energy?

45. How do I deal with my environmental fears?
50. How can I step out of the mass consciousness?
61. What is a spiritual response to a world crisis?
62. How do I deal with the religious conflict in the Middle East?
74. What can I do with the fear I feel over Trump's election?

INDEX of TERMS

A

A Course in Miracles 34, 62, 68, 77, 78, 81
abandon/abandonment 34, 36, 65, 76
acceptance (accept) see themes
addiction 7,26,65
affirm/affirmation 3, 4, 5, 6, 7, 14, 17, 19, 51, 53, 57, 63, 66, 78, 81
ascended master 68, 72, 77, 80
ascension see themes
atone/atonement 4, 8, 79
attachment (attach) see themes

B

being present 40, 57, 73
belief/believe 4, 5, 7, 8, 9, 10, 11, 12, 19, 20, 23, 24, 26, 27, 33, 35, 36, 38, 41, 42, 43, 45, 46, 47, 48, 50, 51, 52, 53, 54, 55, 57, 58, 59, 60, 61, 62, 65, 67, 68, 70, 71, 72, 73, 74, 75, 76, 77 78, 79, 80, 81
belly-mind 43, 44, 45, 46, 56, 57, 58, 59, 60
birthright 7, 24, 30, 32, 39, 51, 60, 72, 76
blame 8, 21, 27, 30, 33, 51, 53, 65, 73, 74, 75, 81
brain-mind 43, 44, 45, 46, 50, 51, 53, 56, 57, 58, 59, 60, 64, 70, 74, 81
Buddha 17, 52, 80
Buddhism 17, 70, 80
Buddhist 27, 28, 47, 80

C

chaos 37, 60, 61
Christianity (Christian) see themes
co-creation 34, 39
commitment (commit) see themes
conscious/consciously 4, 13, 14, 16, 21, 25, 26, 30, 33, 34, 37, 39, 41, 42, 46, 47, 50, 53, 54, 56, 57, 58, 64, 66, 67, 68, 69, 70, 74, 75, 76, 81
consciousness 3, 16, 25, 31, 59, 60, 66, 72

G

H

I

J

making **messages** from
loving hearts
available to a global audience

cocreators @lightspira.com
www.lightspira.com

CPSIA information can be obtained
at www.ICGtesting.com
Printed in the USA
FSOW01n1702210917
38760FS